The Power of Natural Language Processing in Artificial Intelligence

Practical Applications and Deep Learning

S.B. Wade

© Copyright 2024 -Sandra Waite, All rights reserved.

The content contained within this book may not be reproduced, duplicated or transmitted without direct written permission from the author or the publisher.

Under no circumstances will any blame or legal responsibility be held against the publisher, or author, for any damages, reparation, or monetary loss due to the information contained within this book, either directly or indirectly.

Legal Notice:

This book is copyright protected. It is only for personal use. You cannot amend, distribute, sell, use, quote or paraphrase any part, or the content within this book, without the consent of the author or publisher.

Disclaimer Notice:

Please note the information contained within this document is for educational and entertainment purposes only. All effort has been executed to present accurate, up to date, reliable, complete information. No warranties of any kind are declared or implied. Readers acknowledge that the author is not engaged in the rendering of legal, financial, medical or professional advice. The content within this book has been derived from various sources. Please consult a licensed professional before attempting any techniques outlined in this book.

By reading this document, the reader agrees that under no circumstances is the author responsible for any losses, direct or indirect, that are incurred as a result of the use of the information contained within this document, including, but not limited to, errors, omissions, or inaccuracies.

Table of Contents

INTRODUCTION 1
   The Dawn of a Linguistic Revolution in the Age of Machines 1

CHAPTER 1: DECODING THE ABCS OF AI AND NLP 3
   1.1 Untangling the Web of AI 3
   1.2 NLP: Bridging the Gap Between Humans and Machines..................... 5
   1.3 Breaking Down the Jargon: AI and NLP Terminology 7
      Components of Machine Learning 7
      Types of Machine Learning 8
      Applications of Machine Learning 9
      Challenges in Machine Learning 10
   1.4 Addressing Misconceptions: Do You Need a Tech Background to Understand AI? 11
   1.5 Exploring With Examples: Making AI and NLP Tangible 12

CHAPTER 2: A JOURNEY THROUGH TIME: THE EVOLUTION OF LANGUAGE PROCESSING IN AI 21
   2.1 The Dawn of AI: Early Attempts at Language Processing................ 21
   2.2 The Rise of Machine Learning: A Leap Forward in Language Processing.. 24
   2.3 The Era of Deep Learning: The Rise of Sophisticated Natural Language Processing Systems 27
      Progress 28
      Milestones 29
      Challenges 30
      Advancements 32
   2.4 Looking Ahead: The Future of Language Processing in AI 33

CHAPTER 3: DECIPHERING THE LANGUAGE OF MACHINES: HOW NLP WORKS..37
   3.1 How Machines Understand Human Language 37
   3.2 How Machines Generate Human-Like Text 39
   3.3 The Role of Algorithms in NLP 42
   3.4 Unraveling Complex Concepts: Making NLP Accessible................. 42

CHAPTER 4: THE ART AND SCIENCE OF CHATBOTS: MAKING MACHINES TALK 45

4.1 How Do Chatbots Talk? 45
4.2 The Benefits and Limitations of Chatbots 49
    Benefits of Chatbots 49
    Limitations of Chatbots 50
4.3 Building Your Own Chatbot 52
4.4 Ethical Considerations in Chatbot Use 53
4.5 Future of Chatbots 55

CHAPTER 5: UNMASKING EMOTIONS: THE ART AND SCIENCE OF SENTIMENT ANALYSIS 59

5.1 Understanding Sentiment Analysis: More Than Just Words 60
5.2 The Mechanics of Sentiment Analysis: Decoding Emotions 61
5.3 Sentiment Analysis in Action: Real-World Applications 63
5.4 The Challenges and Future of Sentiment Analysis 65
    The Future of Sentiment Analysis 66

CHAPTER 6: BRIDGING LANGUAGES: UNRAVELING THE ROLE OF NLP IN TRANSLATION 69

6.1 Decoding the Language of Machines: How NLP Powers Translation 70
    Understanding the Source Language 70
    Neural Machine Translation (NMT) 70
    Resolving Linguistic Complexities 71
    Tackling Idioms and Cultural Subtleties 71
6.2 Unraveling the Challenges in Machine Translation 72
    Contextual Confusion 72
    Resolving Ambiguities 72
    The Hurdles of Bilingual Data 73
    Innovations: A Ray of Hope 73
6.3 Shaping the Future: The Potential Impact of NLP in Language Translation 73
    Enabling Global Communication 74
    Equalizing Access to Information 76
    Catalyzing Global Business Operations 78
    Enriching Educational Experiences 80
    Ethical and Societal Reflections 81

CHAPTER 7: RIDING THE NEW WAVE: EXPLORING CURRENT TRENDS AND FUTURE POSSIBILITIES IN NLP 83

7.1 POWER OF TRANSFORMER MODELS: CHANGING THE GAME IN NLP 84
7.2 LANGUAGE MODELS GO LARGE: THE EMERGENCE OF LARGE LANGUAGE MODELS 87
7.3 BRIDGING THE GAP: MULTILINGUAL NLP MODELS 88
7.4 THE FUTURE IS HERE: NATURAL LANGUAGE PROCESSING IN THE METAVERSE 89
   Challenges and Ethical Considerations 91
7.5 ETHICS IN THE SPOTLIGHT: RESPONSIBLE USE OF NLP 92
7.6 EMPOWERING WITH NLP: THE FUTURE IS IN YOUR HANDS 94
   It is said that AI and NLP can change the world; is that possible?. 97

CHAPTER 8: REVOLUTIONIZING INDUSTRIES: THE BROAD REACH OF NLP 101

8.1 A PULSE ON HEALTHCARE: NLP AS A DIAGNOSTIC TOOL 101
8.2 THE FUTURE OF FINANCE: NLP IN FINANCIAL FORECASTING 103
8.3 REINVENTING THE CLASSROOM: NLP IN EDUCATION 105
8.4 REVOLUTIONIZING CUSTOMER SERVICE WITH NATURAL LANGUAGE PROCESSING 106
8.5 NLP ACROSS INDUSTRIES: POTENTIAL FUTURE APPLICATIONS 108
   Legal Automation: Simplifying Analysis and Research 108
   Marketing Precision: Tailoring Campaigns 109
   Entertainment Enhancement 110
   The Future of NLP 111
   Creating the Future: Opportunities for Talent 112
   NLP's Promise: Redefining Industries 112
   Potential AI and NLP Future Projects 112

CHAPTER 9: EXPLORING ETHICAL CONSIDERATIONS IN NLP: THE COMPLEX WORLD OF NLP ETHICS 115

9.1 THE PRIVACY PUZZLE: BALANCING UTILITY AND CONFIDENTIALITY 115
9.2 BIAS DETECTION: ENSURING EQUITY IN LANGUAGE UNDERSTANDING 117
9.3 ETHICAL CHATBOT DESIGN: BALANCING EFFICIENCY AND RESPONSIBILITY ... 118
9.4 RESPONSIBLE MACHINE TRANSLATION: RESPECTING CULTURAL SENSITIVITIES
.... 119
9.5 TOWARDS ETHICAL NLP: A CALL TO ACTION 121

CHAPTER 10: NAVIGATING THE AI MAZE: OVERCOMING COMMON CHALLENGES IN NLP 123

10.1 DEMYSTIFYING TECHNICAL JARGON: MAKING COMPLEX CONCEPTS ACCESSIBLE 124
10.2 KEEPING PACE WITH RAPID ADVANCEMENTS: STAYING CURRENT IN THE FAST-EVOLVING WORLD OF AI 125

10.3 BRIDGING THEORY AND PRACTICE: APPLYING AI THEORIES TO REAL-WORLD SCENARIOS 127
10.4 EMBRACING LIFELONG LEARNING: OVERCOMING THE TIME CONSTRAINT IN LEARNING AI 129

CHAPTER 11: MASTERING YOUR NLP JOURNEY: A STEP-BY-STEP GUIDE TO ACTIONABLE AI 131

11.1 CHOOSING THE RIGHT AI TECHNIQUE: YOUR NLP COMPASS 132
11.2 BRINGING YOUR PROJECT TO LIFE: AN NLP IMPLEMENTATION GUIDE 133

CONCLUSION 137

GLOSSARY 139

REFERENCES 149

Introduction

The Dawn of a Linguistic Revolution in the Age of Machines

In an era where machines can paint like Picasso, write like Shakespeare, and compose like Beethoven, we stand at the precipice of a revolution in human-machine interaction, led by the power of natural language processing in artificial intelligence. This is not the distant future; it is the vibrant, pulsating present, where zeroes and ones intertwine with verbs and nouns, creating possibilities that redefine the boundaries of interaction and understanding.

Prepare to journey through a landscape where language becomes a dynamic entity, a conduit through which our conversations with machines transcend the mechanical and enter the realms of enhanced intuitiveness and expressivity. Here, you'll encounter machines that do not just understand the words that we utter or type, but grasp the subtleties of context, the nuances of sentiment, and the rich, varied colors of human intention and expression.

Natural language processing, or NLP, emerges as a hero in our tale, a transformative force that heralds a new age in which the barriers between human language and machine capabilities are not just lowered but obliterated. NLP unleashes the potential for machines to read, understand, and respond to human language in ways that resonate with our natural modes of expression and communication, creating a pathway for more meaningful and contextualized interactions.

This introduction is a starting point that beckons you into a world where the beauty and complexity of human language are celebrated and leveraged to empower technological solutions and applications. In the realm of NLP in AI, language is both art and science, a powerful tool that can be harnessed to drive innovation, enhance experiences, and unlock a spectrum of possibilities in human-machine synergy.

Welcome to an exploration of the extraordinary, where language is unleashed, and the *Power of Natural Language Processing in Artificial Intelligence* stands revealed as a luminary guiding us toward new horizons in technology and interaction. Let us embark together on this exciting exploration, where each page brings new insights, perspectives, and visions of what is possible in the harmonization of human language with the profound capabilities of artificial intelligence.

Chapter 1:

Decoding the ABCs of AI and NLP

As we stand on the brink of a technological renaissance, this chapter demystifies the intricate concepts and terminologies that form the backbone of these revolutionary fields. From understanding the basic building blocks of AI, to unraveling the complexities of NLP, readers will be guided through the fascinating interplay of algorithms, data, and human-like reasoning. This exploration not only illuminates the current state of these dynamic domains but also sets the stage for appreciating their profound impact on our future.

1.1 Untangling the Web of AI

Navigating artificial intelligence (AI) involves exploring ongoing developments in technology and human creativity. AI gives machines human-like intelligence, allowing them to understand, learn, and perform tasks like humans. This exploration covers AI's history, current applications, components, and implications, revealing its innovations, progress, and future potentials.

To begin, we'll explore the key historical milestones that have shaped the evolution of AI, from the groundbreaking Dartmouth Workshop in 1956, which marked the birth of AI as a field, to significant AI breakthroughs that occurred in subsequent decades.

Through real-world examples, we'll showcase how AI has revolutionized fields such as healthcare, where it aids in diagnostics and drug discovery, and finance, where it drives algorithmic trading and risk assessment. We'll highlight its role in transforming transportation with autonomous vehicles and enhancing the entertainment industry with personalized content recommendations.

As we shift our focus to the present, we'll take a look at the contemporary relevance of AI in our daily lives. Ask Siri to play your favorite song, or ask Alexa about the weather; the effortless interaction and accurate responses you receive are testimony to the wonders of AI. These intelligent personal assistants listen, understand, and act upon your commands, showcasing the magnificent capability of machines to replicate human-like intelligence and responsiveness. The seamless integration of AI in virtual assistants like Siri and autonomous systems in vehicles has become routine. We'll explore how AI-driven e-commerce recommendation systems have become integral to online shopping experiences.

Ethical considerations are paramount in the realm of AI. We will address critical issues related to bias in AI algorithms, raising awareness about the importance of fairness and transparency. Privacy concerns in an era of AI-driven data analysis will be discussed, along with the pressing need for responsible AI development practices that prioritize societal welfare.

Finally, we'll peer into the future of AI, considering the potential for general AI to redefine human-machine interactions. The integration of AI in robotics promises to shape industries like manufacturing and healthcare, while AI's role in addressing global challenges, such as climate change and sustainability, presents a compelling vision for the future.

AI presents itself in two predominant forms: narrow AI and general AI. Narrow AI is specialized and task-specific, and excels in executing particular tasks with precision. It's the force behind voice recognition systems like Siri or Google Assistant, and powers the recommendation algorithms that enhance our experiences on platforms like Amazon and Netflix.

Conversely, general AI presents vast possibilities, resembling the advanced AI depicted in movies such as *Ex Machina* and *Her*. Its goal is to replicate a wide range of human-like cognitive functions in machines, allowing them to handle any intellectual task a human can. While general AI remains a subject of future visions and ongoing research, its eventual achievement holds the potential to significantly transform human-machine interaction and capabilities.

We will explore how artificial intelligence intersects with our lives, experiences, and imaginations, uncovering its intricate components.

1.2 NLP: Bridging the Gap Between Humans and Machines

Within the realm of artificial intelligence, natural language processing (NLP) assumes a pivotal role. It acts as a bridge between human language and computer language, facilitating machines' ability to comprehend, interpret, and respond to human communication with precision and relevance.

Think about the simplicity and intelligence behind asking a question to a search engine like Google. Your natural language query is effortlessly understood and answered with accuracy—a testament to NLP's remarkable influence in enabling machines to engage with human language.

NLP also serves as a guardian in the fight against email spam. It can examine email contents, distinguishing between legitimate messages and spam. This showcases NLP's finesse in deciphering textual data.

Moving further into the intricacies of language, NLP demonstrates its versatility and depth. Part-of-speech tagging, for instance, sheds light on words' grammatical roles, revealing whether a word like "apple" represents a fruit or a technology company in a sentence. Another NLP task, entity recognition, identifies proper nouns, including the names of individuals, places, or organizations, within text, providing context and recognition to these entities.

In the domain of emotions and opinions, sentiment analysis takes center stage. It explores text to understand the underlying sentiments or emotions, enriching machines' understanding of human emotional expressions.

On a global scale, machine translation transcends language barriers, facilitating multicultural and multilingual interactions by conveying the essence of thoughts and ideas across linguistic horizons.

In each of these tasks, NLP orchestrates a harmonious understanding and interpretation of human language. It embodies AI's brilliance in the richness and complexity of human communication, bridging the gap between humanity and machines through the artistry of language.

1.3 Breaking Down the Jargon: AI and NLP Terminology

Exploring artificial intelligence and natural language processing involves examining a diverse landscape filled with concepts, methods, and terms. To understand this topic thoroughly, it's important to grasp the basic concepts and key terms associated with it. Knowledge of the foundational principles is essential for further learning and application in various contexts.

In AI, machine learning (ML) is prominent. Machine learning is a subset of AI that focuses on building systems that can learn from and make decisions based on data. Unlike traditional computational approaches that rely on explicit programming to perform tasks, machine learning algorithms use patterns in data to make predictions or decisions without being explicitly programmed to perform the task. For example, think of Netflix using ML to analyze your viewing history and provide tailored recommendations, demonstrating how ML enhances user experiences.

Components of Machine Learning

Machine learning is built upon several pivotal components, each playing a crucial role in the system's ability to learn and make informed decisions. At the heart of this intricate framework is **data**, the foundational element upon which algorithms operate. This data can manifest in various forms, from structured formats like tables and relational databases to unstructured types such as text and images, each offering a unique set of challenges and insights.

The **model** then enters as a mathematical representation, encapsulating real-world processes distilled from the input data. This core component undergoes training using historical data, subsequently being evaluated on its performance and predictive prowess.

Lastly, the **algorithm** acts as the guiding force in this ensemble, comprising the specific computational steps that enable the model to learn from the data. These algorithms are diverse, tailored to suit different tasks including classification, regression, and clustering, providing a structured pathway for the model to evolve and adapt. Together, these components weave the intricate tapestry of machine learning, enabling machines to decipher patterns, make decisions, and offer predictions with increasing accuracy.

Types of Machine Learning

Machine learning, a cornerstone of modern artificial intelligence, manifests in various forms, each distinguished by its approach to learning and interaction with data. **Supervised learning**, one of the primary types, operates on the principle of learning from example. In this paradigm, a model is meticulously trained on a labeled dataset, where each piece of data is tagged with the correct answer or output label. The model's predictions are continuously evaluated, and corrections are made whenever its predictions deviate from the actual outcomes, much like a student learning under the supervision of a teacher.

In contrast, **unsupervised learning** presents a more exploratory approach. Here, the model is set loose on an unlabeled dataset, devoid of specific guidance or correct answers. Its objective is to discern underlying patterns or structures in the data, such as grouping similar data points (clustering) or discovering rules that capture the relationships in the data (association).

The third type, **reinforcement learning**, introduces a dynamic environment where the model, akin to an agent, learns to make a sequence of decisions. It operates through a system of feedback where actions are either rewarded or penalized, thus encouraging the model to devise strategies that maximize cumulative reward.

Collectively, these types of machine learning embody the diverse strategies through which machines can learn, adapt, and potentially outperform human capabilities in various tasks.

Applications of Machine Learning

Machine learning has permeated our daily lives, revolutionizing the way we interact with technology and data. One of the most prominent applications is **predictive analytics**, where machine learning models pore over historical data to make predictions about the future. This has diverse applications, encompassing stock price predictions, weather forecasts, and sales projections, among others, offering valuable insights that aid in decision-making processes.

Another widespread application is in recommendation systems, which have become integral to our online experiences. Whether it's suggesting products on e-commerce platforms, curating personalized playlists on streaming services, or connecting people on social media, these systems leverage user data to provide tailored recommendations, enhancing user engagement and satisfaction.

The field of image and video analysis has seen transformative changes, thanks to ML. Technologies such as facial recognition and object detection are not only augmenting security measures but also enriching user experiences in various sectors, including retail and entertainment, through automatic tagging and personalized content delivery. These applications are just the tip of the iceberg, representing a fraction of machine learning's potential to redefine industries and reshape our future.

Challenges in Machine Learning

In pursuing harnessing the full potential of Machine Learning, practitioners encounter challenges that can significantly impact the performance and applicability of their models. Among these, **data quality** emerges as a critical factor. The adage "garbage in, garbage out" holds true in machine learning; the success of a model is intrinsically tied to the quality, accuracy, and representativeness of the data it is trained on. Inaccurate, incomplete, or biased data can severely undermine the model's ability to make reliable predictions.

Another fundamental challenge lies in balancing the complexity of the model with the complexity of the task at hand, commonly referred to as **overfitting** and **underfitting**. Overfitting occurs when a model is excessively complex, capturing noise along with the underlying patterns in the training data, which leads to poor performance on unseen data. Conversely, underfitting happens when a model is too simplistic to capture the structure of the data, resulting in a lack of robustness in the training data. Both scenarios underscore the delicate act of model selection and the importance of tuning to the specifics of the dataset.

Issues of bias and fairness have come to the forefront, especially as machine learning models find their way into decision-making systems that affect human lives. Models may inadvertently perpetuate or even amplify biases present in the training data or reflect societal prejudices, leading to unfair, unethical, or discriminatory outcomes. Addressing these challenges requires a conscientious approach to data collection, model design, and continuous monitoring, ensuring that machine learning systems perform ethically and justly across diverse scenarios. These challenges, while significant, also present opportunities for innovation and improvement, driving the field towards more robust, fair, and trustworthy solutions.

1.4 Addressing Misconceptions: Do You Need a Tech Background to Understand AI?

Exploring artificial intelligence and natural language processing is often thought of as a journey reserved for tech experts, requiring extensive knowledge of computer science and math. However, we aim to debunk this misconception.

In the world of AI and NLP, knowledge is becoming more accessible to a broader audience. Tools and libraries like Python's NLTK and Scikit-learn have emerged, making AI and NLP more user-friendly and less reliant on complex mathematical algorithms. These platforms allow individuals to harness AI's potential without needing deep expertise in mathematics.

Books play a crucial role in bridging the gap between the mysterious aspects of AI and NLP and the desire for understanding and accessibility. *Make Your Own Neural Network* by Tariq Rashid is an excellent example of such a resource. It simplifies the complexities of neural networks, making the journey less daunting and more about clarity, curiosity, and discovery.

Equipping yourself with a glossary is like having a trusted guide to explain the terminology and jargon, facilitating a deeper understanding of AI and NLP. This clarity ensures that your journey through AI and NLP is marked by comprehension and enriched learning. You will find a limited glossary at the end of this book.

This book embodies a philosophy—a vision that AI and NLP are accessible realms for anyone with a curious mind, regardless of their technological or mathematical background. It serves as a friendly guide, accompanying you on your journey through AI and NLP. The goal is not to intimidate but to enlighten, empower, and foster the joy of exploration and discovery.

1.5 Exploring With Examples: Making AI and NLP Tangible

In our pursuit of understanding of artificial intelligence and natural language processing, real-world examples play a crucial role in clarifying complex theories and concepts. They serve as bridges between abstract ideas and practical applications, making AI and NLP tangible.

For instance, consider how Amazon and Netflix recommend products and movies tailored precisely to individual preferences. Think about voice recognition systems like Siri and Google Assistant, which swiftly understand and respond to human commands. Email spam detection systems tirelessly sift through your communications, distinguishing between wanted and unwanted messages with remarkable accuracy.

AI and NLP are becoming increasingly integrated into everyday life. Here are some common examples:

- Voice Assistants: Voice-activated AI like Siri (Apple), Google Assistant, and Alexa (Amazon) are used for tasks like setting reminders, answering questions, and controlling smart devices.

- Email Filters: Services like Gmail use AI to filter spam and categorize emails.

- Autocorrect and Predictive Text: NLP is used in mobile keyboards to suggest words and phrases while typing.

- Chatbots: Many websites and apps use chatbots for customer support, like virtual assistants that answer common questions.

- Social Media Algorithms: Social media platforms use AI to curate your feed and show relevant ads.

- Search Engines: Search engines like Google use AI to understand queries and provide relevant search results.

- Recommendation Systems: Services like Netflix and Spotify use AI to recommend movies, shows, music, and products based on your preferences.

- Translation Services: Online translation tools like Google Translate use NLP to provide translations between languages.

- Virtual Health Assistants: Some healthcare providers use AI-powered chatbots to provide medical information and appointment scheduling.

- Smart Home Devices: Devices like thermostats, lighting systems, and security cameras can be controlled through AI-based voice commands or smartphone apps.

- Navigation Apps: GPS navigation apps use AI to provide real-time traffic updates and suggest the fastest routes.

- E-commerce Recommendations: Retail websites often use AI to recommend products based on your browsing and purchase history.

- Content Creation: Some news articles, social media posts, and marketing content are generated with the assistance of AI.

- Spam Call Detection: AI-based phone apps can identify and block spam calls.

- Language Learning Apps: Language learning apps often incorporate AI and NLP to provide personalized lessons and pronunciation feedback.

- Accessibility Tools: AI-powered tools assist individuals with disabilities, such as text-to-speech and speech-to-text software.

- Content Moderation: Online platforms use AI to detect and filter out inappropriate content, such as hate speech and graphic images.

- Predictive Text Analytics: AI is used in applications like financial forecasting and predictive maintenance in various industries.

These are just a few examples, and AI and NLP are continually expanding into new areas of our daily lives as technology advances:

- Medical Diagnosis: AI is used to assist doctors in diagnosing diseases and interpreting medical images like X-rays and MRIs.

- Fraud Detection: Financial institutions employ AI to detect fraudulent transactions and protect against cyberattacks.

- Language Translation Services: AI-based translation services like DeepL provide accurate translations for various languages.

- Automated Content Generation: Some news organizations use AI to generate news articles, reports, and financial summaries.

- Manufacturing Quality Control: AI-powered robots and cameras inspect products for defects on assembly lines.

- Virtual Reality and Augmented Reality: AI enhances VR and AR experiences, improving immersion and interaction.

- Environmental Monitoring: AI helps analyze data from sensors to monitor and manage environmental conditions.

- Legal Research: AI assists legal professionals in searching through vast legal databases and documents.

- Supply Chain Optimization: AI optimizes supply chain operations for efficiency and cost savings.

- Personal Finance Management: AI-powered apps offer financial advice, budgeting, and investment recommendations.

- Weather Forecasting: Meteorologists use AI to process large datasets and make accurate weather predictions.

- Agriculture: AI is used for precision agriculture, including crop monitoring, targeted fertilizer application, and automated harvesting.

- Voice Biometrics: AI is used for voice recognition and authentication in security systems.

- Autonomous Vehicles: Self-driving cars rely on AI for navigation and collision avoidance.

- Speech Recognition: AI-powered transcription services convert spoken language into text.

- Emotion Recognition: AI can analyze facial expressions and voice tone to detect emotions used in market research and customer service.

- Robotics: AI-driven robots are used in various industries, from healthcare to manufacturing.

- Energy Management: AI optimizes energy consumption in buildings and industries for sustainability.

These examples showcase the diverse applications of AI and NLP, and the possibilities continue to expand as technology advances. Each application is tailored to address specific challenges and opportunities in different domains.

There are several lesser-known uses of AI and NLP that people may not be fully aware of, including:

- Mental Health Support: AI-driven chatbots and apps are being developed to provide mental health support by offering therapy, monitoring users' emotional well-being, and providing coping strategies.

- Drug Discovery: AI is employed in drug discovery to analyze vast datasets and identify potential drug candidates for various diseases, which can significantly speed up the drug development process.

- Retail Inventory Management: AI helps retailers optimize inventory levels, reducing overstock and out-of-stock situations, improving supply chain efficiency, and ultimately enhancing the shopping experience.

- Disaster Response: AI is used to analyze real-time data during natural disasters to predict their impact, coordinate relief efforts, and assess damage.

- Conversational Agents in Healthcare: AI-powered chatbots assist patients with healthcare information, medication reminders, and symptom tracking.

- Personalized Learning: AI in education tailors learning materials to individual students, adapting content based on their progress and learning styles.

- Legal Contract Analysis: AI can review and analyze legal documents, contracts, and agreements to identify key clauses, risks, and compliance issues more efficiently.

- Astronomy: AI helps astronomers analyze vast amounts of data from telescopes to identify celestial objects, classify stars, and make astronomical discoveries.

- Personalized News Recommendations: AI algorithms customize news feeds based on individual interests, ensuring users receive relevant and diverse news content.

- Scientific Research: AI assists researchers in various fields, from genomics to particle physics, by analyzing data, simulating experiments, and generating hypotheses.

- Energy Conservation: AI optimizes energy consumption in homes and buildings through smart grids and HVAC systems, reducing energy costs and carbon footprints.

- Music Composition: AI-generated music is becoming more prevalent, with algorithms composing original pieces based on style and mood preferences.

- Human Resources: AI helps streamline HR processes by automating resume screening, conducting initial candidate interviews, and analyzing employee engagement.

- Poetry and Creative Writing: Some AI models can generate creative content, including poetry, stories, and artwork.

- Accessibility Tools: AI-powered tools assist individuals with disabilities, such as text-to-speech for the visually impaired and speech recognition for those with mobility challenges.

- Ecological Conservation: AI aids in monitoring and protecting endangered species by analyzing camera trap images, audio recordings, and satellite data.

- Construction: AI assists in project management by predicting project delays, optimizing construction schedules, and enhancing safety on construction sites

Chapter 2:

A Journey Through Time: The Evolution of Language Processing in AI

This chapter embarks on a fascinating historical voyage, tracing the remarkable trajectory of language processing within the realm of artificial intelligence. From the rudimentary symbolic systems of the mid-20th century to the sophisticated, neural network-driven models of today, this narrative explores the relentless drive to create machines that can understand, interpret, and generate human language. As we traverse the decades, we witness the transformation of language processing from a fledgling concept into a cornerstone of AI, a journey that not only reflects the ingenuity of human intellect but also offers a glimpse into the future of human-machine interaction.

2.1 The Dawn of AI: Early Attempts at Language Processing

During the summer of 1956, a significant event occurred in the history of artificial intelligence, known as the Dartmouth

Workshop on Artificial Intelligence, convened at Dartmouth College. This workshop is widely acknowledged as the seminal event that heralded the birth of artificial intelligence as a distinct field of scientific inquiry. The historic gathering had a clear and ambitious objective: to explore the potential of creating computer programs that could replicate facets of human intelligence. The visionaries at this workshop, driven by the belief that machines could be engineered to emulate human thought and problem-solving processes, were at the forefront of a pioneering journey into uncharted technological territories.

In these early stages, the focus of AI research was predominantly on symbolic reasoning and the development of rule-based systems. Pioneers such as John McCarthy, Marvin Minsky, Nathaniel Rochester, and Claude Shannon were instrumental in shaping the field, contributing significantly to the development of early AI programming languages like LISP and delving into the intricacies of logic-based approaches. Concurrently, there was a nascent but notable interest in machine learning. Figures like Frank Rosenblatt were instrumental in this regard, working on early models of neural networks, such as the Perceptron, thereby laying the foundational stones for what would eventually evolve into the complex domain of deep learning.

However, the ambitious goals set by the Dartmouth Workshop were met with a stark reality. The AI capabilities of that era were intrinsically limited by the computational power and data resources then available. Although some early AI programs exhibited rudimentary problem-solving abilities, they were a far cry from the grandiose vision of creating machines endowed with authentic intelligence.

Despite these initial setbacks, the significance of the Dartmouth Workshop in the annals of AI history cannot be overstated. It was this pivotal gathering that charted the course for future exploration and breakthroughs in the field.

The subsequent decades witnessed profound advancements in various domains of AI, ranging from expert systems and natural language processing to robotics, and ultimately to the resurgence of neural networks and deep learning in the contemporary digital epoch. The legacy of the Dartmouth Workshop, therefore, transcends its immediate outcomes, representing a beacon that guided the quest for artificial intelligence, a quest that continues to redefine the boundaries of technology and human potential. While it achieved only limited success, it laid the groundwork for the decades of research and innovation that led to the remarkable advancements in artificial intelligence we see today.

ELIZA, born from the intellectual environment of MIT in the 1960s, emerged as one of the pioneering chatbots of its time. Designed to resemble a psychotherapist, ELIZA engaged in conversations that mimicked human interactions. It crafted questions based on received statements, offering a glimpse into the potential of human-machine interaction. ELIZA's existence served as an early sign of the uncharted territories awaiting exploration in the evolving landscape of technological advancement.

In a parallel narrative, the late 1960s introduced SHRDLU, another creation emerging from MIT's innovative environment. Operating within the controlled confines of a virtual "blocks world," SHRDLU showcased its capability to comprehend and execute commands by selecting and moving different shapes. This demonstration illuminated the potential stages of AI, providing a glimpse of the understanding that AI could achieve within the realm of natural language.

Limitations constrained the initial participants in this linguistic endeavor. They operated within the boundaries of rudimentary computational abilities and simplistic algorithms. They could only perform within a meticulously structured and well-defined language domain. Detailed contexts, rich linguistic landscapes, and subtleties remained uncharted territories. ELIZA, for example, despite its historical significance, struggled with misunderstandings and irrelevant responses because of its limitations in grasping conversational context.

As a result, as the early chapters came to a close, the journey of AI in language processing stood at the cusp of potential. It faced horizons filled with promise but also encountered substantial challenges related to the depth of language understanding and computational capabilities.

2.2 The Rise of Machine Learning: A Leap Forward in Language Processing

With the development of artificial intelligence and natural language processing, machine learning marked a pivotal moment. The 1980s and 1990s bore witness to a transformative act where innovation swept through language processing, revitalizing an AI theater long shrouded in stagnation. Machine learning, which ventured into the realm of data, enabled AI systems to refine their language skills through continuous learning. The machine learning paradigm shattered the constraints of rule-based approaches and introduced data-driven methodologies, facilitating a deeper understanding of linguistic diversity and human expression. AI experts constructed systems capable of continuous learning. Over time and with data input, these systems refined their language skills. Breaking free from rule-based approaches, machine learning introduced data-driven methods, allowing algorithms to adapt to linguistic diversity and understand human expression more effectively.

The era saw the internet's emergence, bringing forth an influx of digital data that enriched machine learning algorithms with a diverse range of content and deep contextual understanding.

Text, spanning from classic literature to real-time news and vast web content, inundated the AI landscape. This empowered AI systems to grasp the complexities of human language, armed with an unprecedented volume of data.

During this transformation, companies such as Google played a significant role in leading innovation in language-related tasks. Google harnessed the power of machine learning to enhance its capabilities, enabling it to excel in tasks like digital searches and translations with increasing agility. Machine learning served as the guiding tool, enabling the search engine to understand user intentions, analyze vast datasets, and uncover valuable and accurate information.

As machine learning gained prominence, the story of AI and language processing was filled with possibilities, transformative techniques, and a journey invigorated by data-driven innovation. However, the story of machine learning in language processing goes beyond these foundational elements. Here are the key facets that have shaped the journey:

- Multimodal Integration: The integration of various data modalities—such as text, images, and audio—has become a defining feature of modern AI systems. This fusion of data types has expanded the horizons of language processing, allowing AI to understand and generate content across diverse media.

- Reinforcement Learning: The application of reinforcement learning, where AI systems learn through interactions and feedback, has played a pivotal role in training chatbots and enhancing language generation capabilities.

- Transfer Learning: Transfer learning, powered by pre-trained language models like BERT and GPT, has revolutionized NLP by allowing models to build on extensive pre-training datasets, significantly accelerating the development of language processing systems.

- Industry Adoption: Beyond technology giants like Google, various industries have embraced machine learning and NLP to improve customer experiences and decision-making processes. Notable sectors include healthcare, finance, and e-commerce.

- Research and Innovation: A vibrant research community, along with academic institutions, has driven machine learning advancements in language processing. Breakthroughs, influential papers, and academic conferences have contributed significantly to the field's growth.

- Ethical Considerations: The dominance of machine learning in NLP has brought ethical challenges to the forefront. Issues related to bias, fairness, copyright law, and responsible AI development have spurred discussions on the importance of ethical guidelines and practices.

Looking ahead, emerging trends, challenges, and potential breakthroughs shape the future of machine learning in NLP. Topics like zero-shot learning, robustness against adversarial attacks, and the collaborative integration of AI with human experts hold promise for the continued evolution of language processing.

2.3 The Era of Deep Learning: The Rise of Sophisticated Natural Language Processing Systems

Deep learning is a subfield of machine learning and artificial intelligence that focuses on using **artificial neural networks** to model and solve complex tasks. It has gained significant attention and popularity in recent years because of its ability to excel in a wide range of applications, from image and speech recognition to natural language processing and autonomous driving.

Artificial neural networks are sophisticated constructs inspired by the human brain. These networks are composed of interconnected layers of artificial neurons or nodes, with each connection featuring an associated weight. The essence of learning in these networks lies in the meticulous adjustment of these weights during the training phase, allowing the network to progressively improve its predictions or classifications.

A distinctive feature of deep learning is its deep architectures, signifying multiple hidden layers within the neural network. Unlike simpler models, deep neural networks boast several layers of "neurons" between the input and output layers, a configuration that empowers them to discern complex and nuanced patterns within the data. The depth of these networks is instrumental to their ability to represent and process data hierarchically.

The training of deep learning models is a data-intensive process. These models are typically exposed to large datasets, a scenario that allows them to learn the intricate mapping between input data and the desired outputs. An algorithm known as

backpropagation, which iteratively adjusts the network's weights to minimize the discrepancy between the predicted outcomes and the actual results, facilitates this learning process. Through this rigorous optimization, deep learning models refine their ability to make accurate predictions or decisions based on the data they are fed.

Deep learning is acclaimed for its prowess in representation learning. Unlike traditional approaches that require manual extraction and selection of relevant features from data, deep learning models are adept at automatically discerning and learning meaningful features and representations directly from raw data. This capacity not only enhances the model's performance but also significantly reduces the time and effort involved in feature engineering, marking a pivotal shift in the way machines understand and interpret the world around them.

Progress

Deep learning has catalyzed significant breakthroughs across various domains, propelling the capabilities of AI to unprecedented heights. In the realm of computer vision, deep learning has demonstrated remarkable proficiency, mastering tasks such as image classification, object detection, and image segmentation. Convolutional neural networks (CNNs), with their unique architecture designed to mimic the human visual system, are at the forefront of these advancements, enabling machines to perceive and understand visual information with astounding accuracy.

The impact of deep learning is equally profound in natural language processing. Here, models like recurrent neural networks (RNNs), long short-term memory (LSTM) networks, and the groundbreaking transformer architectures have revolutionized the way machines understand and generate human language. Transformer architectures, in particular, introduced in the seminal paper "Attention Is All You Need" in 2017, have transformed NLP (Vaswani, 2017). By efficiently harnessing self-attention mechanisms to grasp contextual information, transformers, which can have many layers, embody the true essence of deep neural networks. Their profound impact is evident in a wide array of applications, from machine translation and sentiment analysis to the creation of sophisticated chatbots.

A flagship implementation of the transformer architecture is the generative pre-trained transformer (GPT) series, including the renowned GPT-4 and its successors. These models, pre-trained on colossal datasets, have set new standards in natural language understanding and generation. Capable of being fine-tuned for specific tasks such as text generation, translation, and question answering, GPT models epitomize the pinnacle of NLP, producing text that resonates with human-like nuance and fluidity.

The influence of deep learning extends beyond the confines of text-based NLP. It has made inroads into multimodal applications, where it skillfully analyzes and synthesizes content that amalgamates text, images, audio, and video. This versatility underscores the transformative potential of deep learning, marking a new era where the synergy between humans and intelligent machines fosters unparalleled innovation and creativity.

Milestones

In the ever-evolving landscape of deep learning and natural language processing, certain developments have emerged as particularly transformative, significantly enhancing the interaction between humans and technology. Speech recognition is one such domain where deep learning has made monumental strides. By improving the accuracy and efficiency of speech recognition systems, deep learning has helped to refine technologies, such as voice assistants and transcription services. These advancements not only streamline user interactions with devices, but also pave the way for more natural and intuitive communication, bridging the gap between human speech and machine understanding.

The implications of deep learning extend well into the realm of autonomous systems, marking a revolutionary shift in how machines perceive and engage with their surroundings. Deep learning sits at the heart of developing innovative technologies like self-driving cars, drones, and sophisticated robotics. By equipping these systems with the ability to accurately perceive their environment, deep learning facilitates nuanced decision-making and responsive actions, enabling these autonomous entities to navigate complex real-world scenarios safely and efficiently. This pivotal role of deep learning in autonomous systems underscores its significance in shaping a future where intelligent machines seamlessly integrate into various facets of everyday life, revolutionizing transportation, logistics, and many other industries.

Challenges

The trajectory of deep learning, while marked by groundbreaking achievements, is not without its challenges. One of the most significant hurdles is the need for vast amounts of labeled data to train deep learning models. This requirement often translates into extensive time and resource investments, making the process both costly and labor-intensive. The computational demands of training deep neural networks are substantial. These sophisticated models require powerful computational resources, such as graphics processing units (GPUs) and tensor processing units (TPUs), imposing financial and logistical constraints, especially in large-scale or innovative applications.

Another notable challenge is the inherent lack of interpretability in deep learning models. Often perceived as "black boxes," these models present significant difficulties in deciphering the rationale behind their decisions, complicating the analysis and validation of their actions. This opacity becomes particularly concerning when models inadvertently reflect societal issues, such as biases and disparities, magnifying the ethical implications of AI deployment. The datasets used to train large language learning models (LLMs) may contain considerable amounts of works subject to copyright, which may have been obtained without compensation to authors. Developers must approach AI with a mindset anchored in fairness, integrity, and respect for diversity, ensuring that they conscientiously craft the technology narratives. These instances underscore the necessity.

The environmental impact of deep learning is a multifaceted issue. On one side, deep learning has catalyzed advancements in renewable energy optimization, climate modeling, and resource management, contributing positively to sustainable practices. However, the energy-intensive nature of training deep neural networks, often reliant on data centers with significant carbon footprints, poses a stark environmental challenge. The considerable energy consumption attributed to data processing and storage during model training and inference further exacerbates this concern. Data centers also consume large amounts of freshwater for cooling purposes. As the field progresses, there is an increasing call for innovative solutions aimed at reducing the environmental footprint of deep learning, encompassing more energy-efficient algorithms, hardware optimizations, and eco-conscious computing practices.

In the realm of natural language processing, embracing linguistic diversity has emerged as a pivotal concern. In our interconnected world, fostering effective communication and cultural understanding is crucial for social cohesion, economic progress, and global cooperation. Addressing the nuances of language diversity presents both a challenge and an opportunity for deep learning models to enhance their applicability and inclusivity across diverse linguistic landscapes.

Looking forward, the challenges for deep learning in NLP are manifold. They include refining the models to mitigate biases, enhancing interpretability to demystify the "black box" nature, and innovating towards more energy-efficient architectures. Addressing these challenges is not just a technical necessity but also a moral imperative, ensuring that the advancements in deep learning continue to serve humanity's best interests, aligning with ethical standards and promoting a sustainable and inclusive future.

Advancements

Deep learning has witnessed remarkable advancements, propelling it to the forefront of innovation in artificial intelligence. Key among these advancements are sophisticated architectures such as convolutional neural networks (CNNs), recurrent neural networks (RNNs), generative adversarial networks (GANs), and attention-based transformers. These groundbreaking frameworks have become pillars in a myriad of applications, revolutionizing the way machines perceive, interpret, and interact with the world.

In parallel to these technological strides, there has been a significant surge in collaborative initiatives within the AI community. Researchers and organizations across the globe are joining forces to push the boundaries of what's possible in NLP and beyond. The sharing of datasets epitomizes these collaborative efforts, and the establishment of benchmarks and proliferation of open-source tools are all aimed at collectively advancing the field. The spirit of cooperation and open exchange of knowledge and resources is a testament to the communal dedication to progress in AI.

The influence of deep learning extends far and wide, leaving an indelible mark on various industries. From healthcare and finance to entertainment and autonomous systems, the applications of deep learning are as diverse as they are impactful. With continuous research and development efforts focused on overcoming the challenges and enhancing the capabilities of deep learning, the journey ahead promises to be one of relentless innovation and transformative breakthroughs. The commitment to advancing deep learning not only fuels technological evolution but also paves the way for a future where AI is an integral, beneficial component of every facet of human life.

2.4 Looking Ahead: The Future of Language Processing in AI

The future of language processing in AI paints an exciting picture of what lies ahead for language processing. As we peer into the future, a multitude of key trends and developments are emerging, each signaling the trajectory of AI's evolution. Among these, increasingly advanced models, such as GPT-4 and its successors, stand out. These models are on the cusp of mastering context comprehension, text generation, and the emulation of human-like linguistic patterns with unprecedented precision.

The future also heralds the era of multimodal language understanding. The confluence of various data forms—text, images, audio, and video—will give rise to more holistic AI systems. These systems will adeptly navigate and generate content that interweaves these modalities, paving the way for richer and more dynamic human-AI interactions.

In the domain of conversational AI, we anticipate a significant leap forward. Chatbots, virtual assistants, and conversational AI systems will evolve to engage in more natural, contextually aware dialogues with users. This evolution will transform them into indispensable assets across customer support, information retrieval, and personal assistance.

The field will also witness the proliferation of domain-specific NLP. AI models, tailored to cater to sectors like healthcare, legal, finance, and e-commerce, will burgeon. These specialized models will be finely attuned to the unique challenges and nuances of each industry, delivering bespoke, impactful solutions.

As AI systems grow in complexity, the call for explainable AI (XAI) will grow louder. The pursuit of models that not only make decisions but can explain the rationale behind them will be paramount, especially in sectors where stakes and implications run high, such as healthcare and finance.

Globalization will shape the future of AI, broadening its reach and inclusivity. Efforts will intensify to democratize NLP, ensuring that AI's benefits permeate globally, catering to a diverse tapestry of languages and cultural nuances.

The concept of collaborative AI will also take center stage. In this paradigm, humans and AI systems will collaborate, each augmenting the other's capabilities in research, creativity, and problem-solving, heralding a new epoch of collective intelligence.

In the educational sphere, AI's role will be notably transformative. Language processing AI will spearhead personalized, interactive learning. AI-driven tools will offer instant feedback, translation support, and learning experiences tailored to individual needs and paces.

The future of language processing in AI is a mosaic of innovation, versatility, and ethical consideration. It's a future where AI not only understands and generates text but does so in a way that's more human-like, contextually aware, and ethically grounded. These advancements will not only revolutionize industries and enhance user experiences, but also mark a significant stride in the ongoing journey of AI-driven language processing technology.

In this journey, valuable resources like ArXiv and Towards Data Science can offer guidance, while conferences like NeurIPS and ACL serve as hubs of knowledge exchange. They light the way to a deeper understanding of modern NLP systems. These sources encourage continuous learning, the embrace of evolving insights, and a proactive approach to shaping the future of language processing in AI.

Chapter 3:

Deciphering the Language of Machines: How NLP Works

This chapter examines the intricate mechanisms that enable machines to process, understand, and generate human language. As readers journey through this chapter, they will uncover the fundamental concepts, algorithms, and technologies that make up the backbone of NLP. From parsing text and recognizing speech to sentiment analysis and machine translation, this chapter demystifies how machines interpret the subtleties of language, transforming strings of text and sound into meaningful, actionable information. Prepare to unravel the enigmatic language of machines, gaining insights into the sophisticated world of NLP and its profound implications in our digitally interconnected era.

3.1 How Machines Understand Human Language

Language understanding in machines is a multi-faceted process that starts with the recognition of human speech and extends into the deep analysis of semantics and sentiment. Initially, speech recognition takes precedence, where spoken words are converted into text. Smartphones' speech-to-text features demonstrate a practical integration of this technology in everyday devices, making it a prevalent application.

Entity recognition, coreference resolution, and advanced language models are among the many capabilities that form the bedrock of modern natural language processing. Entity recognition allows machines to discern and categorize entities within text—people, places, organizations, dates, and more—serving as a cornerstone for tasks like information extraction and knowledge graph construction. State-of-the-art language models like GPT-3 and BERT have significantly elevated language comprehension, marking a monumental leap in NLP. These models excel at capturing the nuances of language, recognizing intricate structures and patterns with remarkable proficiency.

Complementing these advancements is coreference resolution, a sophisticated capability where machines identify and link multiple words or phrases in a text that refers to the same entity. This is pivotal for maintaining textual coherence and context integrity. In the auditory domain, emotion recognition in speech has emerged as a groundbreaking technology, enabling machines to decipher and interpret emotions in spoken language. This finds profound applications in mental health support, customer service, and beyond.

The scope of NLP extends to multilingual understanding, enhancing the versatility of machines to comprehend and process multiple languages, catering to diverse global applications. Semantic analysis delves deeper into language comprehension, enabling machines to parse context and relationships within sentences, thus ensuring a nuanced understanding of linguistic intricacies.

Sentiment analysis, another critical component, predominantly serves customer service and social media domains. By analyzing emotional tones in text, businesses glean valuable insights from customer feedback, understanding sentiments towards products or services. Its applications extend to analyzing public opinions on social media, underscoring its indispensable role in modern language processing systems. Collectively, these capabilities not only highlight the sophistication of current NLP technologies but also pave the way for more nuanced and effective human-machine communication.

3.2 How Machines Generate Human-Like Text

In natural language processing, machines have made significant progress in understanding and generating human-like text. Beyond recognizing speech and analyzing semantics, machines can identify entities, use advanced language models, resolve co-references, detect speech emotions, and understand multiple languages. This broad understanding is vital for various applications, from enhancing customer service to improving voice assistant capabilities.

Machines generate human-like text using language models, probability estimation, and contextual understanding. There are several advanced aspects that contribute to the remarkable sophistication of modern text generation technology. To gain a comprehensive understanding of the capabilities and complexities of AI-driven text generation, it is essential to explore its underlying mechanisms and potential applications across various domains.

Language generation is at the heart of how machines produce text that closely mirrors human communication, ensuring that the output is coherent, relevant, and contextually aligned. This involves crafting phrases and sentences in a manner that emulates human speech and writing patterns.

Language models are fundamental in this domain, serving as machine learning architectures that are developed on extensive text datasets. These models operate by estimating the probability of word occurrence based on preceding words within a sentence, facilitating the generation of sequences that exhibit logical and lexical coherence.

Generative adversarial networks (GANs) offer another avenue for language generation. They deploy a dual-network algorithmic approach where one network focuses on generating text, while the other discerns the authenticity of the generated content, achieving a human-like textual output.

An extraordinary capacity for generating text with a striking resemblance to human-written content marks the landscape of modern language models, epitomized by the likes of OpenAI's GPT-3 and GPT-4. These models find their utility across a diverse spectrum of applications, ranging from drafting emails and composing articles to crafting poetry. Their ability to consider not just the preceding words but the entire conversational context elevates the relevance and coherence of their responses, enabling interactions that are more in tune with human communication. This evolution in language generation technology is revolutionizing the way machines produce text, imbuing it with an unprecedented level of fluidity and human-likeness.

To further enhance their performance, these language models undergo a process of fine-tuning, tailored to specific datasets or domains. For instance, a model fine-tuned in medical texts becomes adept at generating content pertinent to the medical field, extending its applicability to specialized sectors. Multimodal capabilities in advanced models have introduced the ability to amalgamate text with other forms of data, like images or videos, enriching the content generated by these machines and enabling them to describe visual content or provide multimedia captions.

Language models also boast the capacity for style transfer, allowing them to emulate various writing styles, voices, or tones—be it formal, casual, or humorous—catering to an array of stylistic preferences. In the domain of creative writing, some AI systems exhibit the ability to weave stories, poems, and other creative compositions, showcasing an alignment with human creativity through neural networks capable of producing imaginative content.

Multilingual proficiency is another hallmark of modern language models, enabling them to comprehend and generate text in multiple languages and serve as invaluable tools for facilitating global communication through translation. These models are designed for real-time interaction, powering chatbots and virtual assistants that engage in instantaneous conversations with users, thanks to the rapid processing and generation of human-like text.

The foundation of many language models lies in transfer learning, a strategy where models, after being trained on extensive datasets, are fine-tuned for specific tasks. This approach allows the models to apply knowledge from one domain effectively in another, enhancing their versatility and applicability. Continual improvement characterizes the field of language processing, with new model versions being constantly introduced, each boasting more enhanced capabilities, refined training data, and superior performance.

However, as machines become increasingly proficient in generating human-like text, it's crucial to navigate the ethical landscape that accompanies these advancements. Issues such as preventing the spread of misinformation and ensuring the responsible deployment of these technologies are at the forefront of the discourse. Researchers and developers are engaged in addressing these challenges, ensuring that the progression of AI text generation technology is aligned with principles of integrity and accountability.

3.3 The Role of Algorithms in NLP

Algorithms are the bedrock upon which natural language processing is built, directing the methodology by which machines process, analyze, and interpret language data. Acting as meticulously detailed recipes, algorithms furnish machines with a sequential procedure to maneuver through tasks.

In NLP, machine learning algorithms are instrumental. They empower models to immerse themselves in text data, absorbing patterns, and internalizing structures, which subsequently inform predictive and decision-making capabilities. A classic illustration is their application in email classification, where algorithms dissect textual features to discern and categorize emails as "spam" or "not spam."

A comprehensive understanding of algorithms goes beyond simply creating NLP applications; it also involves grasping the intricate decision-making processes within these applications. This understanding is essential for effectively troubleshooting and diagnosing issues when an NLP application doesn't perform as expected. Therefore, algorithms are not just operational tools but also crucial instruments for improving comprehension and refining NLP tasks.

3.4 Unraveling Complex Concepts: Making NLP Accessible

Understanding natural language processing can be daunting because of its intricate concepts and terminology. However, there's a way to make these complex ideas more accessible.

Think of a neural network as a busy factory with specialized workers. Each worker contributes to the overall goal by performing their task efficiently and passing it along to the next worker. This collaborative process helps us understand how neural networks operate more clearly.

Imagine an algorithm as a meticulously crafted recipe. Just like a recipe provides a structured roadmap, outlining each step in the culinary creation journey, an algorithm serves as a roadmap, steering machines through their tasks. It precisely coordinates every computational step, leading the machine through processes like sentence comprehension or language translation.

Chapter 4:

The Art and Science of Chatbots: Making Machines Talk

Chatbots exist in the fascinating intersection where technology meets linguistics. Creating and refining these conversational agents is a multifaceted journey, blending the precision of science with the nuance of art. From the initial design to the complex layers of natural language processing, and the continuous evolution driven by AI advancements, this chapter provides a comprehensive exploration of the technologies and methodologies that bring chatbots to life. Prepare to journey into the heart of conversational AI, where the synthesis of art and science transforms the way machines understand, learn, and communicate with us.

4.1 How Do Chatbots Talk?

Chatbots are modern conversational agents that leverage the power of NLP to simulate human-like interactions. The goal is to make the conversation flow, enabling chatbots to not only understand human language but to respond in a manner that is contextually relevant and coherent.

Human language is inherently sophisticated, laden with nuance, contextual cues, and variable meanings, which pose an immense challenge to achieving a realistic and effective human-machine conversation. Despite these obstacles, technological advancements have empowered chatbots like Microsoft's Cortana and Apple's Siri to exhibit remarkable dexterity in comprehending and generating human language, often creating interactions that feel inherently human.

Various refined techniques support the chatbots' linguistic capabilities. A notable one is "intent recognition". This method allows chatbots to glean the user's objective from the provided input, enabling the chatbot to craft responses that are pertinent and satisfying to the user's inquiries or commands. Such a strategy facilitates a better understanding of context, allowing phrases like "What's the weather like?" and "Do I need an umbrella?" to be correctly interpreted as queries about weather conditions.

Further enhancing the efficacy of chatbots is the dynamic process of learning and adaptation, anchored in potent machine learning algorithms. Through continuous exposure to vast troves of conversational data, chatbots can learn, evolve, and fine-tune their responses. This repetitive learning process enables chatbots to mitigate misunderstandings and enhance their interpretative accuracy, continually refining their conversational prowess to provide users with more accurate and contextually aware interactions. Thus, each conversation becomes a building block, contributing to the chatbot's evolving expertise in managing the multifaceted landscape of human language.

Summary of the steps involved in chatbot "Chatting":
- Natural Language Processing: NLP is a key technology that enables chatbots to understand and process human

language. NLP algorithms analyze the user's input to extract meaning and context. This involves tasks such as tokenization (breaking text into words or phrases), part-of-speech tagging, and named entity recognition.

- Intent Recognition: Chatbots use NLP to determine the user's intent—what they want to achieve or the information they seek. For example, a user might ask a chatbot for the weather forecast, which the chatbot recognizes as the intent to get weather information.

- Response Generation: Once the chatbot understands the user's intent and context, it generates a response. This response can be a predefined script or a dynamically generated message based on the user's input. Sometimes, chatbots can use machine learning to improve response generation.

- Language Generation: The chatbot plans a response in natural language, making it sound as human-like as possible. This involves sentence structuring, grammar, and ensuring that the response is coherent and relevant to the user's query.

- Interaction: Some chatbots can engage with users through various modes of communication, including text, voice, and even visual elements, like images or videos. This allows for more versatile and engaging conversations.

- Interface: The chatbot presents the response to the user through a user interface, such as a chat window, a voice interface, or a mobile app. The user can then read or hear the chatbot's response.

- Continuity: Chatbots maintain the flow of the conversation by remembering the context of previous interactions. This allows for coherent and contextually relevant conversations, even if the user's input is ambiguous or fragmented.

- Learning and Improvement: Some chatbots have machine learning capabilities, which enable them to learn from user interactions and improve their responses. This is common in chatbots used for customer support and virtual assistants.

- Feedback: Chatbots may solicit user feedback to assess the quality of their responses and identify areas for improvement. User feedback can be valuable for chatbot developers to refine their algorithms.

Chatbots talk by employing NLP to understand user input, determine intent, generate responses in natural language, and engage users through various interfaces. Chatbots can continuously improve their conversational abilities and provide more accurate and context-aware responses by utilizing AI and machine learning.

4.2 The Benefits and Limitations of Chatbots

Benefits of Chatbots

Chatbots, a revolutionary facet of customer interaction and service, bring forth a multitude of benefits, streamlining operations and enhancing user experiences across various sectors. One of the most significant advantages is their 24/7 availability, ensuring that customer support is a constant service. This is helpful for businesses catering to a global clientele, transcending time zone constraints and providing timely help anytime, anywhere.

In terms of operational efficiency, the cost-efficiency of chatbots is unparalleled. By automating customer service or information dissemination, businesses can significantly reduce the expenses associated with maintaining extensive human support teams. Alongside financial savings, chatbots offer a level of consistency in responses that human agents may struggle to match, guaranteeing that users receive accurate and uniform information during every interaction.

From a scalability perspective, chatbots excel in managing multiple interactions concurrently, catering to a high volume of inquiries without succumbing to delays. This scalability ensures that businesses can maintain quality service even during peak times. The ability of chatbots to provide quick responses helps to reduce wait times, elevating user satisfaction and fostering positive customer relationships.

Beyond these advantages, chatbots are pivotal in the automation of routine tasks such as appointment scheduling, order tracking, and information retrieval. This not only streamlines operations but also allows human agents to focus on more complex, nuanced tasks. The role of chatbots in data collection is also noteworthy; by gathering user data and preferences, they enable businesses to tailor personalized experiences and fine-tune their marketing strategies.

Lastly, chatbots significantly contribute to enhanced user engagement. Through interactive, conversational interfaces, chatbots transform mundane transactions into dynamic, enjoyable interactions, making the user experience more engaging and fostering a deeper connection with the service or brand. Collectively, these benefits underscore the transformative potential of chatbots, positioning them as an integral component of modern business strategy and customer service paradigms.

Limitations of Chatbots

While chatbots offer many advantages, they also come with their own set of limitations that can impact their effectiveness and user satisfaction. One of the primary challenges is their limited understanding of complex or contextually nuanced queries, which can cause inaccurate or irrelevant responses. Chatbots inherently lack empathy and emotional intelligence, making them less suitable for sensitive or emotionally charged conversations where a human touch is crucial.

Language barriers pose another significant limitation, as chatbots are often designed to operate in specific languages, potentially hindering their utility in multilingual environments. Using chatbots raises data privacy concerns, particularly when collecting user data for personalization. Any mishandling of this data can lead to serious security breaches and a consequent loss of user trust.

Regularly updating and refining chatbots to enhance their accuracy and adaptation to evolving user needs, which can be resource intensive, is another challenge posed by the need for continuous training. Despite technological advances, chatbots often still appear impersonal, lacking the warmth and genuineness associated with human interactions.

In terms of capabilities, chatbots have their limitations in problem-solving, especially when faced with complex situations or when creative solutions are required. They are also inherently dependent on technology, making them susceptible to glitches or outages that can disrupt service continuity.

Over-reliance on automation is another concern, as it can lead to diminished human interaction and potentially degrade the overall quality of customer service and relationships. Lastly, ethical concerns emerge, particularly as chatbots may inadvertently reflect and perpetuate biases present in their training data, leading to discriminative responses. Collectively, these limitations highlight the importance of a balanced and thoughtful integration of chatbots, complementing rather than completely replacing human interaction and ensuring ethical and responsible use of AI technology.

Chatbots offer many advantages in terms of efficiency, availability, and scalability. However, they have limitations related to their ability to understand context, provide empathetic responses, and handle complex tasks. Ethical considerations and data privacy are also important factors to address in chatbot deployment. To maximize the benefits of chatbots while mitigating their limitations, organizations should carefully plan their implementation and consider human oversight when needed. Thus, chatbots, for all their efficiency and reliability in certain aspects, are not yet to be considered a full replacement for the depth and adaptability of human communication.

Therefore, while chatbots represent a formidable enhancement in human-machine interactions, they do not wholly eclipse the necessity of human involvement. Their capabilities, although extensive, do not wholly measure up to the subtle understanding, empathy, and adaptability inherent to human interactions.

4.3 Building Your Own Chatbot

Embarking on the journey of building a chatbot is a meticulous process, involving a series of pivotal stages that help to define the functionality and performance of the final product. The journey begins with defining the purpose of your chatbot, a foundational step that involves establishing a clear vision for the chatbot's role. Whether it's handling customer inquiries or aiding in task completion, like booking flights, this defined purpose serves as a guiding light, shaping the chatbot's design and functionality to align with its intended operational role.

Once the purpose is established, we shift our focus to training the chatbot. This stage is critical as it involves equipping the chatbot with the knowledge to interact effectively. Conversational data, which may include previous customer interactions or sample dialogues, acts as the bedrock for this training. This phase is paramount in refining the chatbot's conversational skills and responsiveness.

Simultaneously, crafting responses is another crucial element of the process. Decisions need to be made regarding whether the chatbot will use predefined responses, generate text dynamically based on user input, or employ a combination of both. The chosen strategy significantly impacts the chatbot's interaction quality and the overall user experience.

Using development tools is an integral part of the process. Platforms like Google's Dialogflow and IBM's Watson Assistant have revolutionized the field, providing robust and user-friendly interfaces packed with features that streamline the chatbot development process. These tools have democratized the field of chatbot creation, making it accessible to a wider audience, regardless of their expertise in programming or AI.

By diligently navigating through these stages, developers can create a chatbot that is finely tuned to meet specific needs and capable of engaging in meaningful and effective interactions. The journey, while complex, opens up a world of possibilities for enhancing digital communication and service provision.

4.4 Ethical Considerations in Chatbot Use

Ethical considerations are paramount in ensuring the responsible deployment and use of chatbots, safeguarding user rights and upholding core values. Privacy and data security take precedence, as chatbots often handle personal data to facilitate personalized interactions. It is imperative to prioritize data privacy, transparently communicate data collection practices, and secure explicit user consent for data usage. Implementing robust data security measures, especially in sensitive domains like healthcare, is essential to maintain the confidentiality and security of user information.

Transparency and accountability are also crucial. To prevent any deception or misleading perceptions, we should inform users that their interactions are with a chatbot, not a human, in an unmistakable manner. Ensuring that developers and organizations are accountable for the chatbot's actions and any inadvertent consequences is vital in fostering a trustful interaction environment.

Bias and fairness concerns are significant, as chatbots can inadvertently reflect biases present in their training data. Diligent efforts are required to minimize such biases and guarantee fair responses to all users, irrespective of their race, gender, ethnicity, or other attributes.

User consent is another critical factor. Users should possess the freedom to opt in or out of interactions with chatbots and can discontinue or pause these interactions at any point. Designing chatbots with accessibility in mind ensures that individuals with disabilities can effectively utilize these digital assistants.

Implementing robust monitoring and control mechanisms to oversee chatbot behavior and address inappropriate content or behavior is essential. This also involves providing avenues for users to report any issues. Chatbots should also be transparent about their limitations and disclaimers, clearly communicating the scope of their capabilities and the instances that necessitate human intervention.

Developers must be vigilant in avoiding harm, particularly in critical areas such as healthcare and mental health support, to prevent chatbots from engaging in harmful behaviors or dispensing dangerous advice. The long-term impact of chatbot interactions should also be a consideration, ensuring that they do not inadvertently contribute to social isolation, mental health issues, or other adverse effects.

User education about the functionalities and constraints of chatbots, coupled with clear guidelines on their safe and effective use, is also paramount. Organizations should clearly define data retention and deletion policies to allow users to request data deletion if they discontinue chatbot interaction. Cultural sensitivity should be a focal point in chatbot design to respect language, customs, and cultural norms and avoid offensive or insensitive responses.

Last, continuous monitoring and improvement of chatbot performance based on ethical considerations and user feedback is essential for sustained ethical compliance and user satisfaction. By prioritizing these ethical principles, developers and organizations can ensure that chatbots not only enhance user experiences but also adhere to the highest ethical standards, respecting and protecting user rights and values.

4.5 Future of Chatbots

The horizon of chatbot technology is continuously broadening, propelled by relentless advancements in AI and natural language processing. The future heralds the emergence of chatbots as sophisticated entities, capable of understanding and generating human language with an unparalleled level of accuracy and finesse. These future chatbots will exhibit enhanced linguistic capabilities, engaging in interactions that closely mirror human conversation, adeptly handling complex queries with a nuanced understanding of context and language subtleties.

Future chatbots are expected to develop emotional intelligence in order to humanize digital interactions. They will discern and appropriately respond to users' emotional states, personalizing interactions and making technology more supportive and humane. Experts expect the scope of chatbot applications to dramatically broaden, venturing beyond conventional realms. In mental health support, chatbots could provide compassionate assistance, while in personalized education, they could tailor learning experiences to individual needs and styles.

The dynamic landscapes of AI and NLP offer boundless opportunities for continual learning. Individuals, whether students, professionals, or enthusiasts, will find a rich playground for exploration, learning, and active participation in the evolution of chatbots. Multilingual proficiency will be another hallmark of future chatbots, breaking language barriers and enhancing global communication—an asset in fields like international business, customer service, and diplomacy.

Voice and speech recognition capabilities are ready to evolve and enable users to interact with chatbots through speech instead of text. The integration of chatbots with augmented reality (AR) technologies could provide real-time, context-aware assistance in scenarios like tourism, navigation, or remote troubleshooting.

In healthcare, chatbots could evolve into knowledgeable companions, offering preliminary assessments, medication management, and health advice. They could also serve as companions for the elderly, alleviating loneliness. As comprehensive virtual personal assistants, future chatbots could manage an array of tasks, from scheduling and travel booking to managing finances and providing emotional support.

With the handling of increasingly sensitive data, a heightened focus on privacy and security enhancement will be paramount, ensuring robust protection of user information. The future might also see interconnected chatbots, collaborating to solve complex problems or provide integrated services. AI-enhanced creativity in chatbots could assist users in generating diverse content, while an environmental consciousness in chatbot design could promote sustainability and eco-friendly practices.

In education, enhanced learning and training via chatbots could simulate real-world scenarios, offering personalized learning paths and adapting to individual styles. Cross-platform integration will ensure a seamless user experience across various platforms and devices. Advanced data analytics in chatbots will aid businesses in understanding customer behavior and preferences more deeply.

In times of crisis, chatbots with emergency response capabilities could provide vital support and information. However, the sophisticated advancements in chatbots also necessitate careful consideration of ethical issues, ensuring that technological progress aligns with principles of responsibility, integrity, and user welfare. These prospects underscore the expanding role of chatbots in various life aspects, driven by AI and NLP advancements. Yet, each stride forward will bring its own set of ethical considerations, privacy concerns, and challenges, necessitating a thoughtful approach as technology continues to evolve.

Chapter 5:

Unmasking Emotions: The Art and Science of Sentiment Analysis

This chapter dives deep into the captivating intersection of technology and human emotion, unfolding the complex layers of sentiment analysis, a sophisticated branch of natural language processing that focuses on deciphering the emotional undertones in text. We'll explore the intricate algorithms, linguistic insights, and psychological principles that empower machines to interpret, categorize, and respond to human sentiments. From understanding the basic sentiment of a product review, to unraveling the subtle emotions in literary works, this chapter explains the methodologies and challenges in teaching machines the nuanced art of recognizing emotions. Embark on a journey through the fascinating realm of sentiment analysis, where the analytical rigor of science meets the profound depth of human emotions.

5.1 Understanding Sentiment Analysis: More Than Just Words

Sentiment analysis is a multifaceted field that extends far beyond the mere examination of individual words; it analyzes the elements of language and context to capture the emotional undertones of text accurately. Context is a crucial factor in sentiment analysis, as the meaning and sentiment of words can shift dramatically depending on the surrounding text. For instance, in a car accident, the word "crash" could imply something negative, but when talking about the "crash" of a problematic software application, it might be seen as positive.

The handling of negation is also pivotal, as it can completely invert the sentiment conveyed by certain words or phrases, such as transforming "not good" into a clearly negative sentiment. Emojis and emoticons play a significant role, serving as non-verbal cues that enrich the text with emotional nuances. Sarcasm and irony further complicate sentiment analysis, often requiring a deep understanding of the speaker's intent, as they can convey sentiments opposite to the literal meaning of the words used.

Linguistic ambiguity presents another layer of complexity, with certain words or phrases carrying multiple meanings, each potentially associated with different sentiments. Multi-word expressions, including idioms, also contribute to the intricate nature of sentiment analysis, as the sentiment they convey might not be immediately clear when analyzing the individual words.

Recognizing the subjectivity inherent in language is another aspect of sentiment analysis, acknowledging that not all text expresses clear-cut sentiment, with some statements being neutral or purely opinion-based. Assessing sentiment intensity is also critical, distinguishing between statements with varying degrees of emotional strength.

Cultural nuances are integral to sentiment analysis, considering the cultural and regional variations in language use, where certain expressions might have different connotations across cultures. Domain-specific analysis is equally important, tailoring sentiment analysis to particular industries or fields where specific language use and sentiment expressions prevail.

Advanced sentiment analysis models increasingly employ machine learning and deep learning techniques to capture complex sentiment patterns, taking into consideration multiple facets of language and context. Many organizations opt for customization of sentiment analysis models to enhance accuracy, incorporating domain-specific lexicons and training data tailored to their specific requirements.

Sentiment analysis is a dynamic and intricate process that delves into the nuances of language, context, and emotion. It goes beyond individual words and phrases to capture the sentiment embedded in text data. This makes sentiment analysis an invaluable tool for deciphering public opinion, analyzing customer feedback, and monitoring social media trends, offering profound insights into the emotional landscape of communication.

5.2 The Mechanics of Sentiment Analysis: Decoding Emotions

Sentiment analysis involves a series of intricate steps and techniques. In the first step, known as text preprocessing, the text undergoes cleansing to remove punctuation, special characters, and irrelevant content. To maintain uniformity, text is often converted to lowercase, and tokenization breaks it down into individual words or tokens for more manageable analysis.

Lexicon-based analysis is another cornerstone, relying on dictionaries or lexicons replete with words associated with positive or negative sentiments. Each word in the text is scrutinized, assigned a sentiment score based on its lexicon presence, and these scores are then aggregated to deduce the overall sentiment of the text.

Machine learning approaches take sentiment analysis further, employing models like the naive Bayes classifier, support vector machines (SVM), and recurrent neural networks (RNNs) that are trained on labeled datasets to classify text into sentiment categories. These models adeptly learn from patterns and associations between words and sentiments.

However, analyzing individual words may not fully encapsulate sentiment's context and nuances. N-grams and contextual analysis come into play here, examining sequences of words and surrounding phrases to grasp sentiment in its entirety. Sentiment intensity is also pivotal, distinguishing between the varying strengths of sentiments expressed, quantified through sentiment scores or scales.

Sentiment analysis must also adeptly handle negation and modifiers, reversing or altering the sentiment conveyed by words. Emojis and emoticons are not to be overlooked, as they offer valuable sentiment cues in today's digital communication landscape.

Customization and domain-specific models further refine sentiment analysis, tailoring models and lexicons to specific industries where language and sentiment expressions might differ, enhancing accuracy in domain-specific applications.

To gauge performance, researchers evaluate and validate sentiment analysis models using test datasets with known sentiments. They employ cross-validation and metrics like accuracy, precision, recall, and F1 score. Some applications demand real-time and streaming analysis to keep pace with evolving sentiment trends, using streaming algorithms and tools for continuous monitoring.

The mechanics of sentiment analysis are a blend of linguistic scrutiny, statistical modeling, and machine learning. Despite its advancements, the field continues to grapple with challenges in interpreting sarcasm, irony, and cultural nuances, necessitating more sophisticated natural language understanding techniques.

5.3 Sentiment Analysis in Action: Real-World Applications

Sentiment analysis has emerged as a potent tool, finding extensive applications across a myriad of industries and transforming the way organizations interact with data and understand public opinion. In the realm of social media monitoring, companies leverage sentiment analysis to navigate the vast terrain of platforms like Twitter, Facebook, and Instagram, extracting public sentiment about products, services, and brands. This practice extends to governments and organizations that employ sentiment analysis to gauge public sentiment during pivotal moments like elections, political events, or crises.

In the sphere of customer feedback analysis, businesses scrutinize customer reviews, feedback forms, and online surveys, delving into customer satisfaction and pinpointing areas ripe for improvement. This analysis aids customer support teams in effectively prioritizing and addressing customer complaints and issues.

Sentiment analysis also plays a crucial role in product and service development. Companies harness it to uncover insights about customer preferences, driving product innovation and development while spotting emerging trends and market opportunities. Brand reputation management is another area where sentiment analysis proves invaluable, enabling organizations to track online mentions and news articles to evaluate their brand's standing and empowering PR teams to swiftly respond to adverse publicity or social media trends.

In the financial analysis domain, sentiment analysis is a key asset for parsing news articles, social media posts, and financial reports to understand market sentiment and forecast market trends. Traders and investors utilize this analysis to shape informed trading decisions.

The healthcare and pharmaceutical industry benefits from sentiment analysis too. Healthcare providers analyze patient reviews and feedback to enhance patient experiences and care quality, while pharmaceutical companies monitor patient-reported adverse drug reactions.

In political analysis, sentiment analysis plays a significant role, making it another field where it is heavily employed. Political campaigns and analysts use it to decode public opinion about candidates and issues, and governments apply it to measure public sentiment towards policies and initiatives.

In the movie and entertainment industry, sentiment analysis applies to reviews to assess audience reactions, predict box office success, and fine-tune marketing campaigns based on audience feedback. Customer support chatbots, enhanced with sentiment analysis, offer real-time assistance, adjusting responses based on detected customer emotions like frustration or satisfaction.

E-commerce platforms like Amazon and Netflix deploy sentiment analysis for product or content recommendations, basing suggestions on user behavior and sentiments expressed in reviews. The travel and hospitality sector uses sentiment analysis to refine service quality and identify popular destinations, personalizing travel recommendations to align with individual preferences.

In education and eLearning, sentiment analysis evaluates student feedback on courses and instructors, allowing eLearning platforms to adapt content and quizzes to student sentiments and performance.

These instances underscore the versatile and impactful role of sentiment analysis in driving data-driven decisions, enhancing customer experiences, and offering profound insights across diverse sectors. The capacity to comprehend and react to sentiment in real-time is becoming an invaluable asset in our increasingly data-oriented world.

5.4 The Challenges and Future of Sentiment Analysis

While sentiment analysis has made significant strides in recent years, it still faces challenges that stem from the intricate nature of human language and communication. Contextual understanding is a significant hurdle, as words and phrases often carry different meanings based on their context. Sentiment, inherently nuanced, can be difficult to interpret correctly, making the disambiguation of these nuances a complex endeavor.

Another formidable challenge is the identification of sarcasm and irony. Sentiment analysis models struggle with these linguistic elements as they typically involve words or phrases that, when interpreted literally, convey sentiments opposite to the intended meaning. Data quality and bias further complicates sentiment analysis. Models depend on their training data, and if this data is biased or flawed, the models are likely to generate skewed results. The scarcity of data in multiple languages and dialects can also lead to uneven model performance.

Multilingual sentiment analysis introduces an additional layer of complexity. Each language comes with its own set of linguistic subtleties, cultural references, and sentiment expressions, all of which the models need to accurately recognize and interpret.

Beyond categorizing sentiments as positive, negative, or neutral, emotion recognition presents a more intricate challenge. Distinguishing and categorizing specific emotions like happiness, anger, or sadness demands a more detailed and fine-grained analytical approach.

Last, domain-specific sentiment poses a challenge for sentiment analysis models. Models trained on general datasets often falter in specialized contexts, such as those pertaining to the financial or healthcare sectors. Customizing these models for specific domains is frequently necessary to achieve accurate and reliable results. These challenges underscore the complexity of sentiment analysis and the need for continued research and innovation in the field to enhance the understanding and interpretation of human emotions through technology.

The Future of Sentiment Analysis

Despite the inherent challenges, sentiment analysis is poised for a promising future, driven by continuous evolution and innovation. The trajectory ahead foresees improved accuracy in sentiment analysis models, with advancements in machine learning and deep learning to sharpen their ability to comprehend context, sarcasm, and subtle sentiments more precisely.

The scope of sentiment analysis will broaden with multimodal analysis, integrating data from diverse sources like text, images, audio, and video, paving the way for a holistic understanding of sentiments. Sentiment analysis is expected to advance in emotion detection, becoming increasingly adept at identifying and categorizing specific emotions—a development of immense value in domains such as mental health monitoring and customer service.

Customization will also become a hallmark of future sentiment analysis, with organizations tailoring models to align with their unique industry requirements through domain-specific training and adaptation. Multilingual support is another frontier likely to witness substantial enhancements, enabling businesses to effectively analyze sentiments across multiple languages.

As sentiment analysis integrates deeper into our digital interactions, ethical considerations surrounding privacy, data usage, and bias mitigation will come to the forefront. Ensuring fairness and transparency will be pivotal in addressing these ethical concerns. This progress includes integration with AI chatbots and virtual assistants, refining their capabilities to understand and resonate with user emotions and sentiments.

The demand for real-time analysis will escalate, particularly crucial for businesses and organizations aiming to monitor public sentiment dynamically and respond swiftly in our fast-paced digital landscape. Advances in cross-lingual analysis will break down language barriers, facilitating global marketing efforts and enhancing customer support across linguistic divides.

While sentiment analysis navigates complex challenges related to context, bias, and linguistic intricacies, its future is undeniably bright. As technology forges ahead and the significance of understanding human sentiment escalates, sentiment analysis is expected to play an increasingly pivotal role across a myriad of industries. From marketing and customer service to healthcare and social media monitoring, its influence will be widespread. Navigating the challenges and ethical dimensions judiciously will help to harness the full potential of sentiment analysis and cementing its place in the future of technology and human interaction.

Chapter 6:

Bridging Languages: Unraveling the Role of NLP in Translation

As the world becomes increasingly interconnected, the ability to seamlessly translate between languages becomes crucial, not just for communication but for fostering cultural exchange and understanding. We will explore how NLP stands at the forefront of this linguistic revolution, breaking down barriers and bridging tongues. Readers will journey through the intricate algorithms, machine learning techniques, and linguistic principles that enable the translation of text and speech from one language to another with remarkable accuracy and fluency. Prepare to discover the fascinating interplay between languages and technology, where NLP serves as the bridge, connecting people, cultures, and ideas across the globe.

6.1 Decoding the Language of Machines: How NLP Powers Translation

Natural language processing acts as the formidable engine driving the mechanism of language translation in machines. It represents the technological prowess that fortifies various translation services, most prominently seen in platforms like Google Translate. The role of NLP in translation is quintessential, as it empowers machines to grapple with the complexities of human languages, facilitating the conversion of text from one linguistic medium to another.

Understanding the Source Language

The foundation of translation resides in comprehending the essence and structure of the source language. NLP lends its expertise here by dissecting sentences into more digestible fragments, enabling a granular understanding of linguistic constructs. By analyzing these fundamental components, NLP allows machines to grasp the syntax and semantics of the language, setting the stage for accurate translation.

Neural Machine Translation (NMT)

NMT emerges as a significant innovation, leveraging deep learning to revolutionize the landscape of machine translation. It operates within the realms of pattern recognition, using extensive bilingual text datasets to nurture and refine its translation capabilities. Platforms like Google's Neural Machine Translation (GNMT) epitomize the effectiveness of NMT. GNMT employs a robust neural network architecture that ingests sentences, processes their linguistic attributes, and orchestrates translations that resonate with accuracy and relevance, marking a significant enhancement in the quality of automated translations since its inception in 2016.

Resolving Linguistic Complexities

Despite technological advancements, translation remains an intricate puzzle. It's not merely swapping words between languages, but entails a deeper synchronization with the unique rhythmic and structural flow of each language. All languages have distinctive patterns and styles. For instance, the positional dynamics of subjects, verbs, and objects vary across languages, necessitating a thoughtful realignment and adaptation during the translation process.

Tackling Idioms and Cultural Subtleties

Translation involves dealing with idioms, cultural references, and figurative expressions. These aspects make languages complex and challenging to translate. Translating these elements literally often cannot convey their actual meaning and requires a deep understanding and adjustment to maintain their value across different languages.

NLP is a crucial part of language translation, providing technologies and methods that help understand the complexities of human languages, solving their intricacies, and enabling translation.

6.2 Unraveling the Challenges in Machine Translation

Machine translation, powered by advancements in NLP, has developed significantly. However, challenges remain in linguistic conversion. Despite technological advancements, machine translation has yet to reach the expertise of human translators. This field continuously evolves to improve and enhance translation quality.

Literal translations in machine translation are a common issue. Often, translations are too direct, missing finer details of the original language, resulting in a loss of the full range of meanings and emotions from the original text.

Contextual Confusion

Context is essential for determining meaning in language. Words can have different meanings based on context. Machine translation has difficulty choosing the correct context for conveying meaning. Words with multiple meanings, such as "light", require careful analysis of context to understand whether they refer to weight or illumination.

Resolving Ambiguities

Ambiguities in languages are challenging. Words with multiple meanings make it difficult to determine their correct use in sentences. For example, the word "bank" can refer to financial or geographical terms, making it necessary to understand the context to clarify its specific meaning in a text.

The Hurdles of Bilingual Data

Bilingual data is essential for machine translation. However, this data is not evenly available for all language pairs. Common languages have more bilingual datasets available, while less common languages like English-Welsh have fewer resources. This inequality affects the range and accuracy of machine translation.

Innovations: A Ray of Hope

Innovation and research are enhancing machine translation. Recent developments, such as Facebook's Multilingual Unsupervised and Supervised Embeddings (MUSE), contribute to improvement. This technology allows for direct translations between various language pairs, decreasing reliance on English-focused datasets. It contributes to the progress by supporting languages with fewer translation resources, reducing biases, and increasing accuracy and inclusivity in machine translation.

Machine translation faces various challenges and uncertainties while continually striving to improve and become more precise. Its progress is characterized by ongoing exploration and innovation, which enhances accuracy, context, and nuance in bridging different languages.

6.3 Shaping the Future: The Potential Impact of NLP in Language Translation

The vistas of language translation are being continually reshaped and redefined by the relentless advances in NLP. With each innovative stride, translation technologies inch closer to a future where language barriers crumble, unveiling seamless pathways of global communication and interaction.

Enabling Global Communication

More accurate and precise machine translation technologies are rapidly advancing and poised to usher in a future where language barriers fade into irrelevance, opening unprecedented possibilities for global communication and collaboration. This transformative development in machine translation holds immense potential for breaking down linguistic silos and fostering a world characterized by seamless sharing of ideas, information, and culture across the globe.

Language diversity, with each tongue embodying its own unique culture and thought process, is a cornerstone of our globalized world. Improved machine translation acts as a bridge, connecting these diverse linguistic realms and enabling effortless communication among people from different language backgrounds. This seamless connection fosters not only linguistic but also cultural exchange, as language carries the essence of culture and identity. Advanced translation technologies help to facilitate cross-cultural communication, nurturing mutual understanding and appreciation in a world where the intertwining of cultures is increasingly the norm.

In the realm of business and commerce, the global marketplace thrives on the bedrock of effective communication. Advanced machine translation empowers businesses to expand their horizons, engage with international customers, and explore new markets. It plays a crucial role in enabling multilingual customer support, international marketing, and fostering cross-border partnerships.

In education and knowledge exchange, machine translation emerges as a game-changer. It unlocks a vast reservoir of knowledge and learning materials in various languages, paving the way for academic collaboration across borders and allowing students and researchers to immerse themselves in diverse perspectives.

The media and content localization sector reaps significant benefits from accurate translation. Movies, TV shows, books, and digital content can transcend linguistic barriers, reaching a global audience and fostering cultural exchange and the worldwide dissemination of creative works.

In scientific and technical collaboration, machine translation is indispensable. It streamlines the sharing of research findings, breakthroughs, and technical documentation among international experts, propelling advancements in various fields.

In the realm of humanitarian efforts, effective communication can be life-saving. Relief workers and organizations rely on enhanced translation tools to ensure clear communication of vital information to affected populations during crises.

Machine translation also revolutionized tourism and travel, as it eases language barriers, enriches travel experiences, and encourages cultural exploration. In diplomacy and international relations, the precision of translation is paramount, enabling nations to engage in meaningful dialogue, negotiate treaties, and resolve conflicts by ensuring accurate communication across languages.

In multicultural societies, machine translation promotes community and social integration. It empowers individuals to access essential services, participate in civic activities, and fully engage in their communities, bridging linguistic gaps and fostering a sense of belonging, regardless of their native language.

The advancement of more accurate and precise machine translation technologies marks a transformative shift in global communication dynamics. It paves the way for a world where language diversity is celebrated, and the exchange of ideas, knowledge, and culture knows no linguistic boundaries. This future promises a more interconnected and inclusive global community, where effective communication is accessible to all, fostering cooperation, understanding, and progress on a global scale.

Equalizing Access to Information

Enhancing machine translation has the profound effect of equalizing access to information across linguistic boundaries. This transformation ensures that individuals, irrespective of their linguistic affiliations or proficiencies, can engage with a diverse array of knowledge resources, spanning from news updates to innovative scientific research.

Improved machine translation technology is a pivotal force in breaking down one of the most formidable obstacles to information access: language. It empowers individuals to delve into content in their preferred language, making complex and specialized knowledge more approachable and comprehensible.

In the sphere of current affairs and news, individuals can stay abreast of global events and developments without being hindered by language constraints. News articles, reports, and analytical pieces from across the globe become easily accessible and understandable. This democratization of information extends into the realm of academic and scientific endeavors, where language barriers no longer impede access to research papers, studies, and scholarly publications. Such access not only fosters cross-border collaboration, but also catalyzes the dissemination of knowledge on a global scale.

The field of education also reaps substantial benefits from advancements in machine translation. Students and educators gain access to a wealth of learning materials, textbooks, and academic resources in a multitude of languages, enriching the educational journey and instilling a global perspective in the learning process.

Beyond the realms of academia and current events, machine translation plays a crucial role in promoting cultural exchange. It enables literature, art, and various cultural expressions from diverse regions to reach a wider audience, thus fostering a deeper mutual understanding and appreciation of global cultures.

With economic opportunities, access to a broad spectrum of information is a cornerstone for growth and expansion. By equipping themselves to navigate international markets, decipher market trends, and use business resources in different languages, entrepreneurs and business professionals set the stage for successful global business ventures.

In the healthcare and well-being sector, the availability of medical research, health guidelines, and healthcare information in multiple languages is paramount. Enhanced machine translation ensures that crucial healthcare resources are accessible to a broader audience, contributing to improved health outcomes and well-being.

By dismantling language barriers, advanced machine translation systems help to foster a more inclusive and diverse global community. They promote the inclusion of marginalized communities, ensuring that a wider array of voices is heard and valued. In this way, machine translation not only bridges linguistic divides but also contributes to a more interconnected and empathetic world.

The advancement of machine translation technology serves as a catalyst for equalizing access to information. It empowers individuals across the globe to engage with a wealth of knowledge, spanning various domains, fostering education, cultural exchange, economic opportunities, healthcare access, and a more inclusive and diverse global society. This transformation represents a significant step toward a world where information knows no language boundaries, enriching the lives of people worldwide.

Catalyzing Global Business Operations

Machine translation's enhanced capabilities have the potential to significantly reshape and speed up global business operations in a multitude of ways. In the international business landscape, where efficient communication is crucial, advanced machine translation enables seamless interaction between language barriers. This not only expedites decision-making and collaboration, but also minimizes the potential for misunderstandings, streamlining business operations.

For companies eyeing market expansion, machine translation serves as a valuable ally. By accurately localizing marketing materials, product descriptions, and customer support content, businesses can effectively appeal to new markets, fostering brand credibility and expanding their global footprint.

In the realm of customer support, machine translation proves to be a game-changer. The technology's ability to swiftly translate customer inquiries and offer support in multiple languages not only ensures prompt responses but also showcases a commitment to inclusivity, catering to customers from diverse linguistic backgrounds.

Machine translation also plays a pivotal role in cultivating an inclusive global workforce. By dissolving language barriers within geographically dispersed teams, it fosters enhanced collaboration and synergy, fueling productivity and driving innovation.

Market research and analysis are integral to understanding and navigating international markets. Machine translation aids in the gathering and interpretation of market data, social media trends, and customer feedback from various regions, providing valuable insights into consumer behavior and market dynamics.

Navigating the intricate landscape of international trade involves dealing with legal documents and regulations in multiple languages. Machine translation assists in accurately translating legal contracts, compliance documents, and regulatory updates, mitigating risks associated with legal misunderstandings or compliance violations.

Investing in advanced machine translation systems can lead to substantial cost savings in the long term. Businesses can reduce expenses related to hiring human translators for routine tasks, allowing them to redirect resources towards more strategic aspects of their operations.

In today's globalized economy, businesses leveraging advanced translation technologies gain a competitive advantage. They can respond swiftly to international opportunities, adapt to evolving market conditions, and establish themselves as industry leaders dedicated to effective cross-cultural communication.

Machine translation's refined capabilities have the potential to catalyze global business operations by enabling efficient communication, facilitating market expansion, enhancing customer support, fostering a global workforce, aiding in market research, ensuring legal compliance, delivering cost savings, and providing a competitive advantage. These advantages collectively empower businesses to navigate the complex landscape of international commerce with confidence and effectiveness.

Enriching Educational Experiences

Advanced machine translation has the potential to bring about a profound transformation in education. Imagine a future where language learning is invigorated by innovative technology, offering students and learners a range of powerful tools and resources.

One key advantage lies in the provision of instant feedback. Language learners can receive real-time corrections and suggestions as they practice, enabling them to identify and rectify errors promptly. This immediate feedback fosters a more effective learning process by addressing issues as they arise, accelerating language proficiency.

Translation exercises can also be seamlessly integrated into the learning experience. These exercises go beyond simple word translation and encompass an array of linguistic challenges. Students can engage in activities that involve translating sentences, paragraphs, or even entire texts, honing their translation skills in a practical and interactive way.

Diverse learning aids can be incorporated into language learning platforms. These aids may include multimedia resources, such as videos, audio recordings, and interactive lessons. Such resources not only make learning more engaging, but also cater to different learning styles, ensuring that students have access to a variety of materials that suit their preferences and needs.

In this enriched educational landscape, students can immerse themselves in authentic language contexts. They can explore texts and content from various sources, such as news articles, literature, and academic papers, exposing them to different registers and styles of language. This exposure enhances their comprehension skills and broadens their language horizons.

Advanced machine translation holds the promise of revolutionizing education by offering instant feedback, diverse translation exercises, and a wide range of learning aids. These advancements not only make language learning more effective but also foster a deeper understanding of languages and cultures, enriching the educational experiences of students and learners worldwide.

Ethical and Societal Reflections

The future of machine translation raises ethical and societal concerns. It makes us wonder if the convenience of machine translation might discourage people from learning new languages. Could it lead to the neglect of lesser-known languages and dialects?

We need to explore how advancements in machine translation affect society and culture. It's important to maintain a balanced perspective that values linguistic diversity and ethical considerations. The future of language translation through NLP offers transformation, global integration, and improved communication. However, it also requires us to be mindful of ethical and cultural preservation as we move forward.

Chapter 7:

Riding the New Wave: Exploring Current Trends and Future Possibilities in NLP

This chapter invites readers on an enlightening journey through the dynamic and rapidly evolving landscape of natural language processing. We will uncover the innovative trends that are currently shaping the field of NLP, from advanced machine learning techniques to breakthrough applications in various industries. This exploration does not stop at present advancements; it also casts a forward-looking gaze at the future possibilities, envisioning how NLP will continue to transform our interaction with technology, enhance communication, and redefine our understanding of language and cognition. Prepare to ride the new wave of NLP, where the synergy of language, technology, and human ingenuity promises a future brimming with innovation and boundless potential.

7.1 Power of Transformer Models: Changing the Game in NLP

Transformer models, such as Google's BERT and OpenAI's GPT-3 and GPT-4, have revolutionized the field of NLP, altering the ecosystem with their groundbreaking architectures and capabilities.

BERT has established its niche through bidirectional training, which enhances its ability to understand word context in sentences. This detailed understanding contributes to its excellent performance in NLP tasks such as sentiment analysis, where context comprehension is crucial.

GPT-3 and GPT-4 usher in a new era with their massive architecture, featuring 175 billion parameters. They can generate text with remarkable human-like attributes, creating content that closely resembles human writing. This language generation marks a significant advancement, pushing the boundaries of what's possible in NLP.

Beyond BERT, GPT-3, and GPT-4, there are several other transformer models that have made significant contributions to the field of NLP and related areas. Some of these include:

- Transformer-XL: This model introduced a novel training method that enables learning dependency beyond a fixed length without disrupting temporal coherence. It's effective for tasks requiring an understanding of long-range dependencies.

- XLNet: XLNet outperforms BERT on several benchmarks by using a permutation-based training approach that captures bidirectional context and integrates the best of both autoregressive language modeling and auto-encoding.

- RoBERTa (Robustly Optimized BERT approach): This is an optimized version of BERT, which was trained with more data and for a longer time, leading to improved performance.

- DistilBERT: DistilBERT is a smaller, faster, and lighter version of BERT that retains 97% of BERT's performance while being 40% smaller and 60% faster.

- ALBERT (A Lite BERT): This model provides optimizations that allow for increased performance on tasks while requiring significantly fewer parameters than BERT, making it more efficient.

- T5 (Text-to-Text Transfer Transformer): T5 converts all NLP problems into a text-to-text format, enabling it to perform a wide variety of tasks without significant modifications to the model's architecture.

- ERNIE (Enhanced Representation through kNowledge Integration): Developed by Baidu, ERNIE is designed to improve language understanding by pre-training with knowledge masking strategies, capturing both lexical, syntactic, and semantic information.

- ELECTRA: Instead of masking the input, ELECTRA models are trained to distinguish "real" input tokens from "fake" input tokens (tokens replaced by generator network), which allows them to be more efficient and perform better on smaller datasets.

These models are part of the ongoing development and evolution in NLP, each contributing unique approaches and improvements to the capabilities of language understanding and generation systems. As research progresses, even more advanced models are likely to be developed.

Despite their success, transformer models face ongoing challenges and considerations in NLP and AI. The realm of transformer models, particularly advanced iterations like GPT-3 and GPT-4, require significant computational demands. The extensive resources required for training and inference pose substantial barriers, particularly for individuals lacking access to robust computing infrastructure, such as students, enthusiasts, and hobbyists. While strides are being made towards crafting more efficient models and democratizing access through APIs, the challenges associated with computational demands and associated costs remain formidable.

Alongside these technical hurdles, ethical and practical concerns surrounding the potential misuse of transformer models command serious attention. The prowess of these models in generating coherent, contextually relevant text positions them as potent tools. However, users must pay serious attention to the potential misuse of transformer models, as they have the capability to generate fake news, impersonate others, or create harmful content. Addressing these concerns necessitates the meticulous development and strict enforcement of ethical guidelines and frameworks, a task that has galvanized AI ethicists, researchers, and policymakers into active discourse and action.

Transformer models bring to the fore pressing issues of responsibility, accessibility, and ethics. Questions remain regarding accountability for the harmful content generated by these models, the fair distribution of the benefits they offer, and the mechanisms to mitigate biases in training data that could otherwise perpetuate or amplify unfair stereotypes. The AI community continues to shape the discourse by considering these critical factors. They are committed to ensuring that the development and deployment of transformer models align with principles of responsibility, inclusivity, and ethical integrity.

In summary, while transformer models represent a significant advancement in AI and NLP, they also bring challenges and ethical considerations that require ongoing attention, research, and thoughtful discussion to ensure they are used responsibly and benefit society.

7.2 Language Models Go Large: The Emergence of Large Language Models

The rise of large language models like OpenAI's GPT-3 and GPT-4, as well as Google's T5 marks the current NLP landscape. These vast language models combine scale and capability, constructing coherent and contextually accurate text. They open up new opportunities in NLP, including text generation, summarization, and translation, creating text that is precise and relevant.

In practical applications, large language models can revolutionize traditional learning. Imagine a classroom where a language model helps students write better essays or distill complex texts into concise summaries. These models have the potential to transform education.

However, these language models pose significant challenges. They require extensive computational resources, leading companies to weigh production costs against expected profits. Their size can cause unpredictable and inconsistent outputs. While their autonomous text generation capabilities are impressive, they may sometimes produce inaccurate, inappropriate, or biased content. This raises ethical concerns and the need for safety precautions to ensure responsible use of these tools.

The rise of large language models in NLP signifies significant progress but also prompts consideration of ethics, computation, and responsibility.

7.3 Bridging the Gap: Multilingual NLP Models

In a world where boundaries are continuously being blurred and global interconnections intensify, the role of multilingual NLP models becomes a primary goal. Global integration has amplified the demand for models proficient in multiple languages. Giants in the technology arena, such as Google and Facebook, have committed significant investments to develop models that can use many languages effortlessly and on detailed levels.

Google's Multilingual Universal Sentence Encoder (MUSE) encodes sentences from various languages into a shared conceptual space, enabling cross-lingual tasks like translation and sentiment analysis. MUSE fosters interaction and complementarity among languages, enriching the multilingual landscape.

Developing accurate multilingual models is a complex and challenging journey. Languages are unique and intricate, each with its own structures and nuances. Weaving them together into a cohesive multilingual program requires a detailed understanding of each language's idiosyncrasies and the ability to express them with sensitivity and skill.

Linguistic biases are a significant challenge in the NLP sphere. English, among other widely spoken languages, often receives more resources and attention, creating disparities in the richness and depth of multilingual models. This leaves languages that are less globally prevalent in a space of under-resourced scarcity. To ensure a fairer representation and celebration of linguistic diversity, it is necessary to reevaluate and recalibrate our approaches.

Multilingual NLP models have the potential to promote global integration and understanding. They can help break down language barriers and foster linguistic harmony. However, achieving this vision requires managing the complexities of language with a spirit of equity, inclusivity, and appreciation for the diversity of global languages.

7.4 The Future Is Here: Natural Language Processing in the Metaverse

The world of technology is rapidly evolving, and one of its most exciting frontiers is the metaverse. The metaverse is a collective virtual shared space, merging elements of augmented reality (AR), virtual reality (VR), the internet, and social interaction. In the metaverse, users can engage with each other and digital environments through avatars and experience a persistent virtual world. Companies like Meta (formerly Facebook) have shown a strong interest in developing the metaverse as a new digital frontier.

In the burgeoning realm of the metaverse, NLP stands poised to revolutionize communication and interaction within these virtual worlds. By integrating advanced NLP capabilities, the metaverse can offer more natural and immersive experiences. Features such as voice recognition and real-time language translation enhance the fluidity of communication, while intelligent chatbots stand ready to assist users, making the virtual experience more intuitive and user-friendly.

NLP also plays a pivotal role in content creation and generation within the metaverse. From crafting compelling automated storytelling to generating dynamic dialogue and text-based assets, NLP can inject life into virtual environments, making them more engaging and vibrant.

Personalization and user experience are significantly enriched by NLP. By analyzing and understanding user preferences, NLP can tailor content and interactions within the metaverse, crafting a personalized and immersive journey for each user. This level of personalization ensures that every interaction feels unique and closely aligned with individual user preferences.

On the front of moderation and safety, NLP emerges as a crucial tool. It aids in ensuring a secure and respectful environment within the metaverse by detecting and mitigating harmful or inappropriate interactions and content, fostering a safe and welcoming space for all users.

NLP enhances the sophistication of AI-powered NPCs (non-player characters) in the metaverse. This technology equips NPCs with the ability to engage in more natural and dynamic conversations, enriching the overall quality of interactions and making the virtual world feel more alive and authentic. NLP is not just a tool but a transformative force in the metaverse, redefining the boundaries of virtual communication, creativity, personalization, safety, and interaction.

Challenges and Ethical Considerations

The endeavor of crafting NLP systems for the metaverse is a formidable challenge, demanding a comprehensive and nuanced understanding of human language. This includes a deep appreciation of cultural subtleties, idiomatic intricacies, and the fluidity of context. The architecture underpinning NLP must exhibit both adaptability and depth, proficiently navigating and interpreting the rich tapestry of linguistic expressions with sensitivity and accuracy.

The integration of NLP within the metaverse is not just a technical challenge but also brings to the forefront a spectrum of ethical and privacy concerns. Issues such as data security, potential surveillance, and the risk of misuse are paramount. It's imperative to place a strong emphasis on data protection, ensuring that privacy and security principles are rigorously upheld to safeguard user information within these virtual landscapes. Creating a trustworthy environment where user interactions and data integrity are protected is an essential ethical pillar in the foundation of the metaverse.

In this emerging epoch of technological advancement, guided and shaped by NLP, the metaverse stands as a testament to the potential of virtual worlds enriched with human-like interaction. It envisions a future where virtual realms are not only brought to life by advanced NLP but are also fortified with robust privacy and security measures. In this envisioned future, NLP serves as a bridge in the metaverse, not just connecting individuals but also fostering a deep appreciation for the diversity of language and ensuring the protection of information in these expansive virtual domains.

7.5 Ethics in the Spotlight: Responsible Use of NLP

Ethics and responsible use of natural language processing are essential considerations in the development and deployment of NLP technologies. NLP has the potential to greatly benefit society through the interaction between computers and human language, but it also carries risks and ethical challenges. Here are some key aspects of ethics and responsible use in NLP.

One of the foremost ethical concerns in NLP is bias and fairness. NLP models have the potential to inadvertently internalize and propagate biases present in their training data, leading to outcomes that can be discriminatory. Addressing this challenge, researchers, including teams at institutions like Stanford University, are actively working to devise and implement methodologies that mitigate these biases, such as gender bias, in language models (Kotek et al., 2023). Such endeavors help to foster greater equity within NLP systems.

Transparency in the operation of NLP systems is another critical priority. Both developers and organizations must ensure that users and stakeholders clearly understand how decisions are made by these systems. Striving for algorithms that are explainable and interpretable enhances the trustworthiness and accountability of NLP technologies.

The aspect of privacy is paramount. Given that NLP systems often process and analyze sensitive information, the onus is on responsible usage, which involves robust data protection measures, informed consent from users, and adherence to relevant data privacy regulations. Closely related is security, as safeguarding NLP systems against malicious attacks or misuse is vital. Developers need to be vigilant about potential vulnerabilities and be proactive in securing the technology.

Clear lines of accountability are fundamental for the responsible use of NLP. Organizations must establish mechanisms for addressing any errors, biases, or unintended consequences that arise, including provisions for reporting and rectifying any harm caused.

User consent and control are of utmost importance. Users should be fully informed about how their data is being used and must have the autonomy to opt in or out of specific features or data collection practices. Integrating ethical AI design principles from the very inception of the design process is also crucial. This proactive stance involves contemplating the potential social and ethical impacts of NLP technologies and embedding ethical considerations into the core of the development process.

Adherence to regulations, and compliance with relevant laws, such as data protection and anti-discrimination statutes, is non-negotiable. This ensures that NLP systems operate within the established legal frameworks. Education and training for those involved in the development and deployment of NLP technologies is essential. Staying abreast of evolving ethical standards and responsible practices is imperative in this rapidly advancing field.

Engaging stakeholders from diverse backgrounds, including ethicists, community representatives, and those who are directly impacted by NLP technologies, can provide valuable insights into ethical considerations and help in formulating more comprehensive and inclusive solutions.

Finally, continuous monitoring and evaluation of NLP systems is necessary to identify and address any ethical issues that may emerge. This ongoing vigilance ensures that NLP technologies continue to evolve in ways that are beneficial to society, minimizing potential harm and steadfastly upholding principles of fairness, transparency, privacy, and accountability. Developing and deploying NLP responsibly is a multifaceted endeavor that necessitates a collaborative and multidisciplinary approach, engaging technologists, ethicists, policymakers, and the broader community.

7.6 Empowering With NLP: The Future Is in Your Hands

The future holds great promise for natural language processing, a technology that can transform our interactions with machines and one another. NLP has the potential to enable machines to understand and respond to human language with subtlety and nuance, opening up new possibilities in communication, information access, and global understanding.

The future of NLP is a blank canvas awaiting the contributions of creative minds—students, enthusiasts, and innovators. It encourages individuals from diverse backgrounds to bring their unique perspectives, ideas, and visions to the development of NLP technology.

A series of key advancements promise to transform how we interact with machines. Improved language understanding is at the forefront of these developments, with NLP systems evolving to offer better comprehension and more accurate responses. This evolution will pave the way for more natural, human-like interactions with machines, enhancing accessibility and user-friendliness.

Multilingual and cross-lingual NLP holds immense importance in an increasingly globalized world. The ability to handle multiple languages and facilitate communication across linguistic barriers is crucial for connecting diverse populations.

Future NLP models will also exhibit enhanced context awareness, delving deeper into the context of interactions to provide more relevant and nuanced responses. This advancement will make interactions with AI systems more meaningful and personalized, catering to the unique needs and circumstances of each user.

Bias mitigation will be a focal area of effort, with developers striving to create fairer, less discriminatory models. This involves addressing and neutralizing biases inherent in training data and algorithms, fostering equity and inclusivity in NLP applications.

Conversational AI will become more sophisticated, with chatbots and virtual assistants offering richer, more engaging conversations. This will make them invaluable across a spectrum of applications, ranging from customer support to healthcare.

In the healthcare sector, NLP is poised to play a pivotal role, assisting with medical diagnosis, patient record management, and drug discovery. By providing healthcare professionals with comprehensive, data-driven insights, NLP will contribute to informed decision-making and enhanced patient care.

In education and language, learning will also witness significant enhancements. NLP-powered educational tools will offer personalized learning experiences, supporting learners of all ages in acquiring new languages and skills.

Content generation through NLP will streamline the creation of diverse content types, from writing articles and generating code to composing music, enriching the creative landscape and offering new avenues for creativity.

As the influence of NLP expands, the focus on ethical and responsible NLP will intensify. The development of regulations and guidelines will ensure that NLP systems are developed and deployed ethically, respecting societal norms and individual rights.

NLP will elevate human-machine collaboration, enabling more seamless and productive partnerships between humans and AI systems, especially in areas like data analysis, research, and content creation.

Privacy and security considerations will remain paramount. As NLP systems handle increasingly sensitive data, ensuring the privacy and security of user information will be a top priority, with continuous advancements in technologies to protect and secure NLP applications.

Interdisciplinary integration will see NLP joining forces with other domains, such as computer vision and robotics, crafting comprehensive AI systems that interact with and understand the world in a manner akin to human cognition. This multidisciplinary approach will unlock new potentials and horizons in AI, fostering systems that are more intuitive, responsive, and in tune with human needs and environments.

Many opportunities lie ahead in NLP. You might discover your passion for developing innovative NLP techniques or crafting multilingual models that promote communication in underrepresented languages. There are also ethical challenges to address, such as bias and fairness, as we steer NLP toward a future characterized by moral integrity and universal respect.

The new wave of NLP presents exciting possibilities for those eager to explore the intersections of language and technology. It's a journey of exploration, discovery, and creation, where every contribution shapes the evolution of NLP and its impact on connecting people in a linguistically diverse world.

So, the question for the future is clear: Are you ready to contribute your creativity and vision to NLP's inspiring future?

The canvas is ready, inviting you to illustrate a future where NLP enhances technology with the essence of human language.

It is said that AI and NLP can change the world; is that possible?

The notion of using data to change the world encapsulates the immense potential for data-driven insights and actions in addressing global challenges, enhancing societal well-being, and imparting a positive impact on various facets of life. Data serves as the cornerstone for informed decision-making across diverse sectors such as public policy, healthcare, education, and business, enabling decision-makers to discern trends, evaluate outcomes, and make choices conducive to improved results.

In public health, data helps to monitor disease outbreaks, tracking vaccination rates, and pinpointing health disparities. Particularly during pandemics like COVID-19, data-driven models are crucial for predicting the spread of the virus and shaping public health strategies.

Environmental conservation also benefits significantly from data. Information gleaned from sensors, satellites, and environmental monitoring devices is pivotal in informing conservation efforts, helping to track ecosystem changes, identify endangered species, and combat climate change through evidence-based policies.

Data is invaluable in disaster response, bolstering disaster preparedness and response capabilities. It powers early warning systems for natural disasters, enables real-time crisis monitoring, and steers resource allocation to impacted areas.

In education, data analytics plays a key role in assessing student performance, pinpointing learning gaps, and customizing educational content to individual needs. This data-driven approach aids educators in refining teaching methods and boosting student outcomes.

Financial inclusion is another area where data makes a significant difference. Leveraging data, especially through credit scoring models based on alternative data sources, broadens access to financial services for underserved populations.

Data-driven analysis is also a potent tool in promoting social justice, uncovering inequalities and biases within systems such as criminal justice, employment, and housing, and advocating for fairer policies and practices.

In business and innovation, data-driven insights are pivotal in shaping business strategies, optimizing supply chains, and enriching customer experiences. It catalyzes innovation by identifying market trends and discerning consumer preferences.

Data is equally critical in planning and executing humanitarian aid, especially in crisis situations. It enables organizations to target resources strategically and assess the impact of their interventions.

In the sphere of research and scientific discovery, data accelerates progress by providing a wealth of information for experiments, simulations, and analyses, leading to breakthroughs in domains like genomics, astronomy, and materials science.

Government transparency benefits from open data initiatives that enhance government accountability and public scrutiny. Publicly available data allows for the assessment of government performance, tracking of expenditure, and fostering of civic engagement.

Global development initiatives, such as the United Nations Sustainable Development Goals (SDGs), rely on data to gauge progress toward targets and pinpoint areas needing attention.

As data usage expands, the importance of data privacy and ethics escalates. Protecting individual privacy and ensuring ethical data practices is imperative. Evolving regulations and ethical frameworks aim to safeguard data while maximizing its potential benefits.

Data empowers citizens to participate in decision-making processes and hold institutions accountable. Civic tech initiatives leverage data to create platforms that facilitate citizen engagement, closing the loop in a comprehensive approach to using data to change the world.

In summary, using data to change the world involves leveraging the vast amount of information available to address complex challenges, foster innovation, and create positive societal change. However, it also requires responsible data governance, ethical considerations, and collaboration across sectors to ensure that data-driven efforts have a lasting and beneficial impact on the world.

Chapter 8:

Revolutionizing Industries: The Broad Reach of NLP

This chapter ventures into the expansive and transformative impact of natural language processing across various sectors. NLP is not just a technological tool but a revolutionary force, reshaping the landscape of industries from healthcare to finance, education to customer service, and beyond. From automating customer interactions to extracting insights from vast datasets, NLP is proving to be an indispensable asset in the digital age. Prepare to journey through the realms of industry, discovering the profound influence and limitless potential of NLP in revolutionizing business practices, decision-making, and customer engagement.

8.1 A Pulse on Healthcare: NLP as a Diagnostic Tool

In the healthcare industry, NLP is emerging as a pivotal force, significantly enhancing care delivery, analytical precision, and support mechanisms. The technology's adeptness in interpreting patient records is revolutionizing diagnosis and therapy, elevating both speed and accuracy.

Initiatives like Zephyr Health's Unlocking Clinical Insights are at the forefront of this transformation. Startups like Zephyr Health are harnessing the power of NLP to revolutionize diagnostics by meticulously analyzing complex clinical and financial data. This not only uncovers invaluable insights but also expedites diagnoses, diminishes errors, and markedly improves patient outcomes.

In the sphere of mental health, NLP is manifesting as a compassionate ally. Chatbots such as Woebot, equipped with cognitive-behavioral therapy techniques, offer a level of support that transcends traditional therapy boundaries. These chatbots provide readily accessible support, making mental health care more inclusive.

NLP's predictive proficiency is opening new horizons in identifying health risks. Researchers at esteemed institutions like Boston Children's Hospital are using NLP to sift through electronic health records, predicting risks like suicide tendencies (Pearl, 2023). This predictive prowess enables timely and potentially life-saving interventions.

Google's DeepMind epitomizes the predictive and preventative potential of NLP in healthcare. By analyzing patient records, DeepMind predicts medical issues such as kidney injuries, embodying a proactive approach to healthcare that emphasizes prevention and precision.

NLP's transformative role in healthcare is undeniable. It heralds a future where diagnostics are not only accurate but also faster, where care is empathetic, and life-saving predictions are a reality. Across its myriad applications, NLP is a catalyst for innovation, enhancing accessibility and effecting a profound impact in the healthcare sector.

8.2 The Future of Finance: NLP in Financial Forecasting

NLP is at the helm, steering the industry towards unprecedented innovation and efficiency, setting the future of finance and financial forecasting for a transformative shift. NLP's capacity for advanced data analysis is a game-changer, adeptly mining insights from a wealth of unstructured financial data, such as news articles, earnings reports, and social media sentiments. These insights offer a deep dive into market sentiment, investor behavior, and economic trends, paving the way for informed decision-making.

NLP's prowess in delivering real-time insights is revolutionizing the finance sector. Financial professionals, armed with NLP-powered algorithms, can now interpret news and social media data as events unfold, ensuring they remain at the forefront of market developments and make astute, timely decisions.

Risk management is another domain where NLP is making its mark. By pinpointing potential risks and anomalies in financial data, NLP enhances the capacity of financial institutions to assess credit, market, and operational risks with heightened precision.

Companies like Bloomberg are pioneering the use of NLP in navigating the stock market (Bloomberg Professional Services, 2023). Using NLP's analytical acumen, they can analyze an array of news articles and social media trends to forecast stock prices with nuanced precision. NLP's ability to map out patterns, discern sentiments, and decode market moods equips investors with a comprehensive understanding, guiding their financial forecasting and investment strategies.

In the realm of algorithmic trading, NLP informs strategies by scrutinizing news and financial reports to identify market-moving events, while also gauging sentiment around specific assets or industries. Meanwhile, NLP-driven chatbots and virtual assistants are revolutionizing customer service and chatbots in banks and financial institutions. These innovative solutions answer inquiries, provide account details, and assist with financial planning, blending convenience and functionality to streamline customer interactions.

NLP's role in regulatory compliance is equally significant. It assists financial institutions in navigating the complex landscape of regulations by analyzing and categorizing extensive regulatory documents and legal texts. NLP's capabilities extend to earnings forecasting, leveraging textual data from earnings calls, news articles, and reports to refine earnings forecasts and shape investment strategies.

In the critical area of fraud detection, NLP stands as a vigilant guardian. Companies like Mastercard employ NLP to analyze the language nuances in customer communications and transaction descriptions, uncovering potentially fraudulent activities and bolstering financial integrity and consumer trust.

NLP supports portfolio management by offering insights into news and sentiment related to specific assets or sectors, aiding portfolio managers in making astute investment decisions. Financial institutions are also leveraging NLP to provide personalized financial advice, tailoring recommendations to individual clients based on their financial goals, risk tolerance, and prevailing market conditions.

On a global scale, NLP's proficiency in global market analysis is invaluable, offering a panoramic view of financial news and reports from around the world, and unveiling potential investment opportunities.

As NLP continues to reshape finance and financial forecasting, ethical considerations remain paramount. Ensuring that NLP algorithms are unbiased and transparent is an ongoing priority, underscoring the importance of ethical technology deployment.

The future of finance, powered by NLP, is on the cusp of significant growth and innovation. NLP's nuanced understanding of human language is proving to be an indispensable asset for financial institutions, investors, and individuals alike, enabling them to navigate the complex financial landscape with informed confidence and effective risk management.

8.3 Reinventing the Classroom: NLP in Education

In education, natural language processing is emerging as a transformative partner, cultivating rich and diverse learning experiences. Some areas improved by NLP are: language acquisition, writing integrity, and personalizing learning pathways. NLP promotes innovation and enhancement in the educational ecosystem.

Language Learning: Real-Time Feedback Mastery

In language learning, innovative apps such as Duolingo excel at providing learners with immediate, sophisticated feedback on their pronunciation and grammar. Duolingo has the remarkable ability to listen attentively to spoken words, assessing pronunciation accuracy and analyzing the intricacies of grammatical structures. As learners engage with the app, it offers them a live, real-time reflection of their language performance, coupled with clear pathways for refinement and improvement.

Essay Grading: Preserving Authenticity and Excellence

In essay composition, EdTech's Turnitin employs NLP to uphold the principles of integrity and quality. In assessing the essays, Turnitin ensures that the ideas conveyed are authentically crafted, reflecting genuine thought and expression. Turnitin goes beyond the surface to refine the content and writing style, ensuring that the final essay product strikes a balance that aligns seamlessly with the lofty standards of academic excellence.

Personalized Learning: Tailoring Education to Unique Needs

In educational innovation, startups like Century Tech lead to personalized learning. They use NLP and AI to tailor content to each student, reshaping traditional teaching. This approach involves precise content adjustments and pacing for individual needs, replacing one-size-fits-all methods. Century Tech customizes content based on each learner's strengths, weaknesses, and preferences, enabling personalized learning that nurtures potential.

8.4 Revolutionizing Customer Service With Natural Language Processing

In today's digitally-driven business landscape, customer service has undergone a significant transformation, thanks to integrating NLP technology. NLP is rapidly revolutionizing the way companies interact with their customers, providing a more efficient, personalized, and responsive approach to customer support.

One of the key advantages of NLP in customer service is its ability to understand and process natural language, enabling automated systems to engage in meaningful conversations with customers. This means that customers can interact with chatbots or virtual assistants in a manner that feels natural, as if they were speaking to a human agent. This level of sophistication not only enhances the overall customer experience but also frees up human agents to handle more complex and high-value tasks.

NLP-powered systems can analyze vast amounts of customer data in real-time. They can identify trends, sentiments, and common issues that customers are facing. This valuable insight enables businesses to proactively address customer concerns and make data-driven decisions to improve their products or services.

NLP can streamline routing customer inquiries to the right department or agent, reducing wait times and ensuring that customers receive quicker responses to their queries. This efficiency not only improves customer satisfaction but also helps businesses optimize their operational costs.

NLP-driven analytics can provide valuable feedback on customer interactions. Businesses can analyze conversations to identify areas where agents may need additional training or support, leading to continuous improvement in customer service quality.

Natural language processing is revolutionizing customer service by enabling businesses to provide more personalized, efficient, and data-driven support. As NLP technology continues to advance, it promises to reshape the way companies engage with their customers, creating a win-win situation where customers receive better service, and businesses benefit from improved customer satisfaction and operational efficiency.

8.5 NLP Across Industries: Potential Future Applications

As we look to the future of technology, NLP takes center stage, illuminating industries with its transformative capabilities. From legal chambers to marketing and entertainment, NLP brings efficiency, personalization, and strategic prowess to various sectors.

Legal Automation: Simplifying Analysis and Research

In the legal arena, technology companies such as ROSS Intelligence have harnessed the power of NLP to revolutionize the way analysis and research are conducted within the realm of legal documents. NLP, in this context, serves as an invaluable tool that goes beyond mere automation. It effectively streamlines and expedites the traditionally labor-intensive and time-consuming tasks associated with legal research.

NLP-driven systems possess the remarkable ability to scan, comprehend, and meticulously extract pertinent information from extensive legal databases, statutes, case laws, and legal precedents. This comprehensive understanding of legal language and content allows for rapid document indexing, context analysis, and the identification of relevant clauses, significantly reducing the hours typically spent on manual research.

NLP-enabled automation extends beyond simple data retrieval. It can provide insights by identifying patterns, trends, and anomalies within legal texts, enabling legal professionals to make informed decisions. By simplifying complex legal language and distilling it into actionable insights, NLP enhances the efficiency of legal operations, ultimately saving valuable time and resources.

Because of this streamlined and efficient approach, legal professionals are liberated from exhaustive document review, allowing them to redirect their focus towards strategic analysis, client counseling, and case preparation. This not only speeds up the legal decision-making process but also enhances the quality of legal services, as attorneys can now dedicate more attention to understanding the nuances of cases, strategizing effectively, and providing personalized guidance to clients.

Marketing Precision: Tailoring Campaigns

In marketing, integrating natural language processing represents a strategic shift that goes far beyond mere customization. NLP serves as a data-driven powerhouse, enabling marketers to craft campaigns with unparalleled precision and relevance.

NLP-driven systems excel in the analysis of vast datasets, examining consumer behaviors, preferences, and historical interactions. This analytical prowess allows for a comprehensive understanding of the target audience's psyche. By examining linguistic cues and patterns in customer interactions, NLP finds out not only what customers say but also what they truly mean. This level of insight goes far beyond surface-level data and allows marketers to make informed decisions.

Predictive analytics, powered by NLP, enable marketers to predict consumer behavior with remarkable accuracy. By recognizing trends and identifying potential opportunities, NLP equips advertisers with the ability to stay one step ahead of their target audience. This strategic advantage allows for the creation of campaigns that are not only timely but also highly effective.

With this depth of understanding, marketers can craft messages that resonate on a personal level. NLP-driven systems can generate content that aligns with individual preferences, tailoring the message to each recipient's unique interests and needs. The result is a marketing campaign that feels less like an advertisement and more like a personalized message, which significantly increases its persuasive impact.

NLP's real-time capabilities allow for agile campaign adjustments. Marketers can track and analyze ongoing campaigns, making instant modifications based on changing consumer sentiment or emerging trends. This flexibility ensures that marketing efforts remain highly responsive and adaptive to the ever-evolving landscape.

Entertainment Enhancement

In the entertainment industry, the application of NLP has ushered in a new era of content curation, one that is finely attuned to the detailed preferences and emotions of viewers. Platforms like Netflix have emerged as pioneers in this field, leveraging NLP to revolutionize how content is selected and presented to their vast audience.

NLP's role in entertainment enhancement begins with its capacity to analyze vast amounts of textual and conversational data from diverse sources. By combing through social media chatter, reviews, and even casual conversations, NLP can gauge the pulse of audience sentiment. It discerns not only what viewers are discussing but also the emotional tone associated with their conversations. This level of insight is invaluable for content providers seeking to create emotionally resonant experiences.

NLP can analyze the content of scripts, dialogues, and narratives within shows and movies. By dissecting the linguistic and emotional nuances embedded in the storyline, NLP can gauge the potential impact of content on viewers. It identifies themes, tones, and character interactions that are likely to resonate, allowing for content recommendations that align with the audience's emotional predispositions.

The result is a content recommendation system that goes beyond surface-level genre preferences. NLP empowers streaming services like Netflix to suggest shows and movies that are not just based on broad categories but on the specific emotional states viewers are seeking. Whether it's heartwarming dramas, thrilling adventures, or laugh-out-loud comedies, NLP ensures that the content presented resonates with the viewer's current mood or desired emotional experience.

NLP's real-time adaptability ensures that recommendations remain in sync with evolving viewer preferences. The application of natural language processing has ushered in a new era of content curation, finely attuned to the nuanced preferences and emotions of viewers. As viewers engage with content and provide feedback, the system continually refines its understanding of their tastes. Platforms like Netflix have emerged as pioneers in this field, leveraging NLP to revolutionize how content is selected and presented to their vast audience.

The Future of NLP

As AI technology continues its rapid evolution, natural language processing stands as a dynamic and versatile tool with the potential to bring about transformations across various industries. NLP's growth and development in recent years has underscored its ability to offer precise and adaptable solutions, making it a pivotal component in the ever-expanding landscape of artificial intelligence. As it continues to advance, NLP holds the promise of delivering transformative impacts across sectors because of its unparalleled accuracy and versatility.

Creating the Future: Opportunities for Talent

In this evolving era of NLP, opportunities abound for both aspiring and seasoned professionals, as well as students eager to make their mark in natural language processing. The growing demand for NLP expertise opens doors for individuals to contribute their creativity and innovation to this dynamic domain. By embracing the intricacies of NLP, they can play a crucial role in shaping its future and driving innovation within an ever-evolving technological landscape.

NLP's Promise: Redefining Industries

Its capacity for innovation, efficiency, and strategic mastery roots the promise of NLP to redefine industries in the future. Across sectors, from healthcare to finance and beyond, NLP is poised to reshape traditional practices, enabling seamless collaboration between technology and language. As this symbiotic relationship unfolds, industries will embark on a journey of exploration, discovering new possibilities and harnessing the power of NLP to streamline processes, enhance decision-making, and revolutionize the way they operate.

Potential AI and NLP Future Projects

The future of NLP and AI is teeming with exhilarating possibilities, and while forecasting specific, unprecedented applications remains a challenge, a wave of emerging trends and potential future applications is on the horizon. Emotionally intelligent AI is at the forefront of this wave, poised to transform mental health support, customer service, and personal assistance by understanding and responding to human emotions with heightened sensitivity.

In the healthcare industry, AI for drug personalization will revolutionize treatments by tailoring medications to individuals' genetic profiles and health histories. AI's role in scientific discovery is equally promising, with AI-driven research in biology, chemistry, and materials science expected to expedite breakthroughs and foster innovation.

The creative industries are not left untouched; AI-enhanced creativity is emerging as a collaborative force alongside artists, writers, and musicians, pushing the boundaries of human creativity. In law enforcement, advanced AI systems are expected to refine the analysis of surveillance data, predict criminal behavior, and bolster public safety, all while navigating the complex terrain of privacy concerns.

AI's transformative influence extends to the educational sector with AI-generated personalized education, where AI-powered platforms are envisioned to adapt to individual learning styles and needs, offering bespoke learning experiences. In journalism, AI-enhanced journalism may assist in data analysis, fact-checking, and generating investigative reports.

Space exploration is yet another frontier for AI, with AI-powered robots and spacecraft set for autonomous exploration of remote celestial bodies. In healthcare, AI-driven healthcare diagnosis could significantly enhance the accuracy and speed of medical condition diagnosis, alleviating the burden on healthcare systems.

AI-managed ecosystems will play a pivotal role in monitoring and managing biodiversity, combating climate change, and protecting natural resources. AI in language revitalization could prove instrumental in preserving and reviving endangered languages.

Disaster preparedness is another domain where AI could make a significant impact, improving the prediction and mitigation of natural disasters. AI in personalized nutrition will offer dietary recommendations tailored to individual health data, genetics, and dietary preferences, while AI for autonomous agriculture could revolutionize farming practices through AI-controlled drones and robots.

In the fashion industry, AI in personalized fashion is expected to recommend clothing and accessories based on personal style, body measurements, and current trends. Meanwhile, AI in quantum computing is expected to solve complex problems at unprecedented speeds by working alongside quantum computers.

Human-machine collaboration is poised to see AI systems augmenting human capabilities across various industries, enhancing productivity and efficiency. AI-powered personalized medicine and AI-enhanced environmental monitoring will offer customized treatments and sophisticated climate change assessments, respectively.

AI in advanced robotics promises groundbreaking applications in healthcare, manufacturing, space exploration, and disaster response. While these future applications are speculative and contingent on technological progress, ethical considerations, and societal acceptance, the continuous evolution of AI and NLP heralds a future replete with innovative solutions, addressing challenges and unlocking new opportunities across a diverse array of domains.

Chapter 9:

Exploring Ethical Considerations in NLP: The Complex World of NLP Ethics

Natural language processing has many applications in various domains, such as information retrieval, machine translation, sentiment analysis, chatbots, and more. However, NLP also poses many ethical challenges and dilemmas, such as bias, privacy, copyright violation, fairness, accountability, and social impact. In this chapter, we will explore some of the ethical considerations in NLP, and discuss how to address them in a responsible and ethical manner. We will also examine some of the existing frameworks and guidelines for NLP ethics, and highlight some of the open questions and future directions in this complex and important field.

9.1 The Privacy Puzzle: Balancing Utility and Confidentiality

In natural language processing, a critical challenge lies in the delicate balance between harnessing extensive text data for its immense potential, and ensuring the confidentiality of sensitive information. NLP stands out in its ability to analyze vast arrays of text data, driving forward innovations in sectors like healthcare. For example, patient records can reveal insights, aiding in the prediction of disease patterns and crafting personalized medical strategies, holding the promise of saving lives.

However, the use of such data demands a conscientious approach, especially in sensitive areas like healthcare analytics. Personal data privacy, including patient records, is paramount. We must relentlessly anonymize data, preserving the confidentiality and dignity of individuals. This unwavering dedication to privacy forms the ethical bedrock for handling sensitive data.

In the sphere of customer service, NLP-powered chatbots have become ubiquitous, celebrated for their efficiency and quick responses. Yet, these chatbots bear the crucial responsibility of protecting user data. Key principles, which include collecting only what data is necessary, storing data with robust security measures, and handling user data with the highest respect and caution guide this responsibility.

Transparency is a cornerstone of building trust within ethical NLP practices. It's imperative for users to have a lucid understanding of how their data is used. Take language learning platforms such as Babbel or Rosetta Stone, where NLP not only provides personalized feedback but also enhances the learning experience. Users should be cognizant of the fact that their text inputs are analyzed in a manner that safeguards privacy and enriches their educational journey.

In summary, while NLP harbors immense potential, its sustainable success is contingent upon a steadfast commitment to balancing utility with confidentiality, ensuring a responsible and respectful approach within the NLP landscape.

9.2 Bias Detection: Ensuring Equity in Language Understanding

Bias in NLP is a nuanced challenge, capable of leading to unfair outcomes and reinforcing harmful stereotypes. For instance, AI recruitment tools can perpetuate biases if their training data lacks diversity.

To combat bias, it's crucial to prioritize diverse and representative data in NLP systems. This helps create an equitable ecosystem, even in sophisticated systems like Google's search engine, which can occasionally reveal biases in search results.

Diversity plays a vital role in addressing bias. Assembling diverse teams to develop NLP systems is essential for ethical practices. These teams bring a wealth of perspectives and insights, helping uncover and mitigate biases lurking in algorithms and data.

Detecting and mitigating bias in NLP is an ongoing journey. It requires continuous vigilance to uphold principles of inclusivity and respect, ensuring NLP systems promote equity and fairness.

Addressing bias in NLP involves a coordinated effort, from embracing diverse data to nurturing diverse human perspectives, to move the field toward fair horizons.

9.3 Ethical Chatbot Design: Balancing Efficiency and Responsibility

Ethical chatbot design focuses on creating chatbots that balance efficiency and responsibility while adhering to ethical principles. It involves developing chatbots that not only provide effective interactions but also prioritize ethical considerations in their design and operation.

Key aspects of ethical chatbot design include:

- Transparency: Ensuring that chatbots clearly communicate their non-human nature to users, avoiding deception and promoting trust.

- Authenticity: Balancing crafting chatbot interactions that resemble human-like responsiveness and maintaining an ethical stance that respects the boundaries of truthful representation.

- Data Privacy: Safeguarding the personal information shared during chatbot interactions, protecting it from misuse or unauthorized access.

- Responsible Use: Using data and information shared during interactions in a responsible and ethical manner, with respect for user privacy and consent.

- Bias Mitigation: Implementing measures to detect and mitigate biases in chatbot responses to ensure unbiased interactions with users.

- User Well-Being: Prioritizing the well-being of users by promoting positive and helpful interactions and avoiding harm or negative consequences.

- Diverse and Inclusive Design: Ensuring that chatbots are inclusive and considerate of diverse user backgrounds, needs, and preferences.

Ethical chatbot design seeks to create AI-driven conversational agents that not only perform tasks efficiently but also uphold ethical standards, respect user privacy, and promote responsible and trustworthy interactions. This balance between efficiency and responsibility is essential in building chatbots that contribute positively to user experiences while respecting ethical principles.

9.4 Responsible Machine Translation: Respecting Cultural Sensitivities

Responsible machine translation is a multifaceted endeavor that revolves around the careful consideration of cultural sensitivities. It encompasses a range of practices and principles aimed at ensuring that machine translation systems not only provide accurate translations but also respect the cultural nuances and intricacies inherent in languages.

At its core, responsible machine translation recognizes the profound connection between language and culture. Every language reflects the culture it originates from, embodying its values, beliefs, customs, and history. As such, a responsible approach to machine translation involves going beyond the literal translation of words and phrases and delving into the cultural context that underlies the language.

One key aspect of this responsibility is the avoidance of any translation that might unintentionally offend, misrepresent, or marginalize specific cultural groups. Training machine translation systems to recognize potentially sensitive terms, idiomatic expressions, or cultural references is essential. They should provide translations that are not only linguistically accurate but also culturally appropriate.

Responsible machine translation entails considering the diversity within cultures. Different regions, communities, or even individuals within a culture may have unique linguistic preferences or sensitivities. Therefore, a responsible translation system should allow for customization or adaptation to accommodate these variations, ensuring that the translations align with the specific needs and expectations of different user groups.

This might involve providing alternative translations, offering explanations of cultural references, or flagging potentially sensitive content for human review. It's about creating a system that can navigate the delicate balance between linguistic accuracy and cultural sensitivity, ultimately fostering intercultural respect, understanding, and effective communication.

Responsible machine translation is about more than just linguistic accuracy; it's about honoring cultural sensitivities and recognizing the inseparable link between language and culture. By adopting responsible practices, machine translation systems can contribute to bridging cultural gaps and promoting respectful and effective cross-cultural communication.

9.5 Towards Ethical NLP: A Call to Action

"Towards Ethical NLP: A Call to Action" represents a critical and timely initiative within the field of natural language processing. It signifies a collective acknowledgment of the ethical considerations that are increasingly vital as NLP technologies continue to evolve and permeate various aspects of our lives. This call to action underscores the imperative for the NLP community, including researchers, developers, policymakers, and users, to come together and address ethical challenges proactively.

One primary focus of "Towards Ethical NLP" is the recognition of potential biases and ethical dilemmas that can arise in the development and deployment of NLP systems. NLP technologies inherit biases present in the data on which they are trained when interacting with human language and communication. These biases can manifest as discriminatory outcomes in various applications, from language translation to content recommendation. Acknowledging these biases is the first step in rectifying them and ensuring that NLP technologies operate equitably.

Another key aspect of this call to action involves promoting transparency and accountability in NLP systems. Users of NLP technologies should clearly understand how these systems work, how they make decisions, and what data they use. Transparency not only builds trust but also allows for scrutiny and accountability when issues arise. It encourages responsible development and use of NLP systems.

"Towards Ethical NLP" emphasizes the importance of robust ethical guidelines and standards in the NLP community.

This call to action also recognizes the role of education and awareness in fostering ethical NLP practices. It encourages educational institutions and organizations to incorporate ethics into the NLP curriculum and to raise awareness among developers and users about the ethical considerations and potential pitfalls of NLP technologies.

"Towards Ethical NLP: A Call to Action" represents a pivotal moment in the evolution of NLP. It urges stakeholders to unite in addressing ethical challenges, from bias mitigation to transparency and accountability, and to work collaboratively towards a future where NLP technologies enrich our lives while upholding ethical standards and principles. It serves as a rallying cry for responsible innovation and ethical stewardship within the NLP community.

Chapter 10:

Navigating the AI Maze: Overcoming Common Challenges in NLP

Embarking on a journey through the intricate labyrinth of artificial intelligence, this chapter delves deep into the realm of natural language processing, unraveling the complex web of challenges that practitioners frequently encounter. As we navigate this convoluted terrain, we uncover the multifaceted obstacles that range from linguistic nuances and contextual ambiguities to the ethical quandaries posed by data privacy and algorithmic transparency. This chapter serves as a guide, offering insights and strategies to maneuver adeptly through these hurdles, paving the way for the effective and ethical implementation of NLP solutions. By confronting these challenges head-on, we aim to harness the full potential of NLP, transforming it from a perplexing puzzle into a powerful tool that enhances communication and understanding in the age of AI.

10.1 Demystifying Technical Jargon: Making Complex Concepts Accessible

Making complex concepts accessible is a crucial endeavor aimed at bridging the gap between specialized technical knowledge and broader understanding. In an increasingly technology-driven world, technical jargon and complex concepts often act as barriers, preventing people from accessing and comprehending important information and innovations. This initiative acknowledges the importance of breaking down these barriers to promote inclusivity, effective communication, and informed decision-making across diverse audiences.

One of the central goals of demystifying technical jargon is to simplify intricate technical concepts into language that is easily digestible by non-experts. Whether it's explaining artificial intelligence, blockchain, quantum computing, or any other complex topic, the initiative seeks to present these subjects clearly. This involves using plain language, relatable analogies, and real-world examples to make the content relatable and accessible to a broader audience.

This initiative recognizes that accessibility extends beyond just simplifying language. It also involves considering various learning styles and preferences. To cater to diverse audiences, we can present content in different formats, such as written articles, infographics, videos, or interactive demonstrations. This multi-modal approach ensures that individuals with varying learning preferences can engage with and understand technical concepts.

Besides breaking down complex concepts, this teaching style places a strong emphasis on fostering a culture of curiosity and lifelong learning. It encourages individuals to ask questions, seek clarification, and engage in open discussions about technical topics. This initiative promotes continuous learning and empowers individuals to expand their understanding of complex subjects by creating an environment where questions are welcomed and knowledge-sharing is encouraged.

The initiative also underscores the importance of collaboration between technical experts and communicators. Effective communication of complex concepts often requires a partnership between subject experts who possess the technical knowledge and communicators who excel at making that knowledge accessible. This collaborative approach ensures that accurate information is conveyed without losing its depth and integrity.

Teaching and learning using plain language is a vital initiative that champions accessibility, inclusivity, and effective communication in the realm of complex technical subjects. By simplifying language, employing diverse formats, encouraging curiosity, and fostering collaboration, this initiative helps break down barriers and empowers individuals from all backgrounds to engage with and understand complex concepts, contributing to a more informed and technologically literate society.

10.2 Keeping Pace With Rapid Advancements: Staying Current in the Fast-Evolving World of AI

AI is in a constant state of flux, characterized by a whirlwind of advancements and innovations that can often seem overpowering. However, it is essential to adapt strategies in order to smoothly sail through this storm of rapid developments, staying relevant and updated. Here's a guide to help navigate the swift currents of this dynamic field:

Engaging with Informative Media

- Blogs and Articles: Platforms like the *Towards Data Science* blog offer a wealth of knowledge presented in digestible formats. Regular engagement with such blogs can aid in grasping new concepts and staying abreast of recent advancements.

- Consuming content from sources like the *Artificial Intelligence (AI) Podcast* and channels such as *Two Minute Papers* is a way to seamlessly incorporate learning into one's daily routine. These sources curate and present information in engaging ways that make learning feel less cumbersome.

- Participating in online communities

- Platforms like Reddit's Machine Learning subreddit and Stack Overflow's AI section act as bustling hubs for AI enthusiasts. Participation in these communities fosters a culture of shared knowledge, facilitating discussions, clarifications, and real-time updates from diverse participants in the AI field.

- Enrolling in online courses

- Coursera, edX, and Other Platforms: Online learning platforms such as Coursera and edX offer meticulously structured courses that mirror the pulse of the current AI landscape. Enrolling in these courses presents an opportunity to delve deep into a subject via structured learning pathways, guided by updates and curated contents reflective of the latest in AI and NLP.

Staying current in the world of AI necessitates a commitment to continuous learning and adaptation. By employing these strategies, one can hope to keep pace with the rapid advancements, ensuring that your knowledge remains relevant and fresh in this ever-evolving landscape.

10.3 Bridging Theory and Practice: Applying AI Theories to Real-World Scenarios

Embarking on the journey from theoretical knowledge to practical application in AI can often seem daunting. However, a step-by-step, structured approach can facilitate this transition smoothly, turning challenges into valuable learning experiences. Below are strategies and insights to bridge the gap between theory and practice in AI.

Start Small: Simplify to Amplify

- Simple Applications and Projects: Begin with uncomplicated projects that allow the application of learned concepts in a real-world context. For instance, crafting a basic sentiment analysis program using Python libraries like TextBlob or NLTK to analyze Twitter tweets is a practical way to begin. These minor projects act as a foundation, building confidence and reinforcing learned theoretical concepts.

Engage in Competitive Learning

- Coding Challenges and Hackathons: Platforms such as Kaggle act as arenas where you can apply, test, and hone your AI skills. Engaging in these competitive environments with real-world datasets and challenges provides practical experience and the opportunity to learn from a broader community. It not only enhances problem-solving skills, but also fosters a competitive spirit that can be highly motivational.

Leverage the Open-Source Community

- Use Open-Source Libraries: The open-source community is a treasure trove of resources. Libraries like TensorFlow and PyTorch are not only free to use but also come with the flexibility of modifications as per project requirements. Leveraging these resources not only facilitates the application of theoretical knowledge but also encourages learning from the global community and contributing back to it.

Continuous Learning and Application

- Consistent practice and application of knowledge in various practical scenarios are vital. Continuously seeking opportunities to apply theories, be it through minor projects, competitions, or leveraging open-source resources, ensures steady progress and enhancement of skills.

Transitioning from theoretical AI knowledge to its practical application is a journey of continuous learning and adaptation. Simple projects, competitive learning platforms, and the open-source community offer invaluable resources to navigate this path successfully, turning theoretical knowledge into practical wisdom and skills.

10.4 Embracing Lifelong Learning: Overcoming the Time Constraint in Learning AI

Learning AI, or any substantial technical skill, can often seem like an overwhelming task because of perceived time constraints. However, with strategic planning and the adoption of a conducive mindset, one can overcome these challenges, making learning an integral and manageable part of daily life.

Adopt a Lifelong Learning Mindset

- Continuous Journey: Treat learning AI not as a destination but a journey. Just as with acquiring a new language, learning AI requires persistent effort, practice, and the mindset of continuous exploration. Embracing a lifelong learning approach ensures sustained growth and adaptability in the ever-evolving field of AI.

Seamlessly Integrate Learning into Daily Routines

- Life offers pockets of time that can be used for learning. Simple strategies, such as listening to a relevant podcast during a commute or engaging with a blog post during lunch breaks, can effectively integrate learning into daily routines, making it less daunting.

Harness the Power of Online Learning Platforms

- Flexible Learning Paths: Platforms like Khan Academy, Coursera, and Codecademy have revolutionized learning by offering flexibility. These resources allow for self-paced learning, ensuring that you can plan and undertake your studies in a manner that aligns with your schedule and pace, reducing the pressure and making learning more enjoyable.

Practical Application and Regular Practice

- Consistency is Key: Regular engagement with the learning materials and consistent practice are essential. By dedicating time regularly, even in smaller segments, one ensures that learning becomes a habit rather than a task, enhancing retention and mastery.

Overcoming time constraints in learning AI is a matter of strategic integration of learning into daily life and adopting a flexible and continuous learning mindset. Using available resources wisely and maintaining consistent engagement ensures that learning AI becomes a manageable, enjoyable, and ultimately rewarding endeavor.

Chapter 11:

Mastering Your NLP Journey: A Step-by-Step Guide to Actionable AI

We now embark on an expedition into the heart of natural language processing, offering a comprehensive, step-by-step guide designed to transform novices into adept practitioners of actionable AI. This chapter demystifies the complexities of NLP, presenting a clear and actionable roadmap that spans from foundational concepts to advanced applications. Readers will navigate through the intricacies of algorithm selection, data preprocessing, model training, and beyond, all while being equipped with practical tips and insights to overcome common pitfalls. Whether you're looking to refine your skill set or implement NLP solutions effectively, this chapter serves as your quintessential compass, guiding you through the evolving landscape of AI with clarity and confidence.

11.1 Choosing the Right AI Technique: Your NLP Compass

Effectively, choosing the best AI techniques for your NLP requirements and goals relies on handling the intricate array of options available.

- Align Techniques With Goals and Data Nature: Prioritize aligning the selected AI technique with your specific objectives and the inherent characteristics of your data. Different tasks call for various techniques. For instance, handling vast text data might benefit significantly from sentiment analysis or topic modeling. Conversely, unraveling the structure of sentences might necessitate techniques such as dependency parsing or part-of-speech tagging.

- Develop a Comprehensive Understanding: Cultivate an understanding of each AI technique's strengths and constraints. Acquainting yourself with this knowledge enables a strategic selection process, enhancing your project's success likelihood. For example, neural networks, while potent, might not always be the optimum choice, especially for straightforward tasks, because of their substantial data and computational resource demands.

- Adapt to Your Resources: Adapt your technique selection based on resources. Simpler models like decision trees or linear regression might be apt choices when dealing with limited data or computational power, promoting a more efficient and workable approach.

- Continuous Learning and Adaptation: Commit to an ongoing learning process to stay abreast of the latest AI advancements and innovative techniques. A continuous learning approach ensures your methods remain current, relevant, and optimized for evolving challenges and opportunities in NLP. Employ multiple avenues like reputable AI blogs, webinars, conferences, and online courses to keep your knowledge base fresh, expansive, and forward-thinking. By embracing a thoughtful, informed, and adaptive strategy in choosing AI techniques, you can traverse the NLP landscape with a sense of direction, precision, and confidence, ensuring that your projects are both successful and impactful.

11.2 Bringing Your Project to Life: An NLP Implementation Guide

Implementing an NLP project is an exhilarating opportunity to bring your knowledge to fruition and witness the remarkable capabilities of natural language processing in action. As you embark on this journey, you'll follow a structured process that takes your project from a mere concept to a functional and reliable NLP solution.

A. Define Clear Project Goals

Your journey begins with a crystal-clear definition of your project's goals. These objectives will act as your guiding star throughout the implementation process. The goals you set will determine the scope and direction of your NLP project. Consider the diverse applications NLP can have, such as analyzing customer feedback, creating chatbots, or extracting insights from textual data.

For example, if your project involves building a chatbot for your website, start by outlining the specific details. What kind of questions will it answer? What tone should it employ to engage users effectively? How will it handle unexpected or ambiguous queries? Defining these goals lays the foundation for the subsequent steps in your NLP implementation journey.

B. Gather and Prepare Data

Gathering and preparing data is a pivotal step in your NLP project. The quality and quantity of your data directly impacts the performance of your NLP model. Data collection may involve web scraping, using APIs, or aggregating existing datasets. Once collected, your data must undergo rigorous cleaning and preprocessing.

For instance, if you're working on sentiment analysis of Twitter data, you'll start by collecting tweets using Twitter's API. Next, you'll clean the data by removing irrelevant information, special characters, and noise. Preprocessing may also include tasks like stemming, simplification, and encoding the text to numerical values suitable for modeling. Finally, your dataset should be divided into training and test sets, ensuring that your model can be effectively trained and evaluated.

C. Build and Test Your Model

The heart of your NLP project lies in building and testing your model. This phase is where you put theory into practice and choose the appropriate AI techniques based on your project's goals and data characteristics, as discussed in detail in section 11.1.

For example, if your project revolves around sentiment analysis, you may opt for a technique like logistic regression for its simplicity or delve into more advanced approaches like neural networks for enhanced accuracy. Your choice of algorithm will depend on the complexity of your NLP problem and the data.

Rigorous testing is crucial once you construct your model. This involves using your designated test dataset to evaluate how well your model performs. Metrics like accuracy, precision, recall, and F1-score can assess its effectiveness in meeting the project goals.

Implementing an NLP project is a gratifying journey that takes you from ideation to realization. Through clearly defined goals, meticulous data preparation, and thoughtful model selection and testing, you can bring your NLP project to life with confidence and success.

Conclusion

In closing, our exploration of natural language processing has illuminated the transformative power of this field within the realm of artificial intelligence. NLP has emerged as a pivotal force, reshaping industries and redefining the way we interact with technology and information. As we conclude this journey, let's recap the key takeaways that underscore the significance of NLP in our rapidly evolving world.

NLP Unleashes the Potential of Language: NLP empowers machines to understand, interpret, and generate human language. This ability opens doors to a myriad of applications, from chatbots that assist customers to sentiment analysis that deciphers public opinion.

Structured Implementation Is Vital: Building an NLP project demands meticulous planning. Clearly defining project goals, gathering and preparing data, and selecting appropriate AI techniques are foundational steps to ensure success.

Lifelong Learning Is Essential: NLP is a dynamic field where change is constant. Staying current with the latest advancements, reading research papers, attending conferences, and engaging with online communities are vital practices for those seeking mastery.

Embrace Complexity and Growth: Rather than being daunted by the complexity of AI and new technologies, see them as opportunities for growth. Every small step forward is progress, and every new tool is a chance to enhance your NLP projects.

A World of Possibilities Awaits: NLP's potential is boundless. Whether you aim to improve customer service, automate tasks, or gain insights from unstructured data, NLP offers a wealth of opportunities to innovate and make a meaningful impact.

In parting, we encourage you to continue your journey into the captivating world of NLP. As the field continues to evolve, so too does its capacity to transform industries, solve complex problems, and enrich our lives. Embrace the challenges, remain curious, and never stop exploring the horizons of natural language processing.

Thank you for embarking on this NLP adventure with us. Here's to your continued learning, growth, and success in the dynamic world of NLP and artificial intelligence.

Dear Reader,

I am writing to request your valuable expertise and insight for a book review of *The Power of Natural Language Processing in AI: Practical Applications and Deep Learning*.

Your insights as a reviewer would be immensely valuable in helping potential readers understand the content, relevance, and impact of this book. Your review will contribute to the broader discussion surrounding NLP and AI, making it an invaluable resource for those interested in technology, language processing, and AI applications.

Your feedback and critique will be greatly appreciated.

Thank you for considering this request, and I look forward to the possibility of your review contributing to the ongoing dialogue about NLP and AI.

Warm regards,

SB Wade

Glossary

AI Bias: Unfair or discriminatory outcomes in AI systems, often due to biased training data or algorithms.

AI Chatbot Ethics: The ethical considerations and guidelines for the development and use of AI-powered chatbots, including transparency, privacy, and responsible AI practices.

AI Chipsets: Specialized integrated circuits or chips designed to accelerate AI computations and improve energy efficiency in AI applications.

AI Ethics: The study and application of ethical principles in the development and use of artificial intelligence.

AI Explainability: The ability to understand and interpret the decisions and predictions made by AI models, especially in complex deep learning models.

AI Fairness: Ensuring that AI systems are designed and trained to avoid discrimination and treat all individuals or groups fairly.

AI Governance: The establishment of policies, regulations, and guidelines for the ethical and responsible use of artificial intelligence.

AI Hardware: Specialized hardware components, such as Graphics Processing Units (GPUs) and Tensor Processing Units (TPUs), designed to accelerate AI model training and inference.

AI in Agriculture: The application of AI for tasks like crop monitoring, precision farming, and pest control in agriculture.

AI Model: A representation of a real-world process or system, typically created using machine learning, that can make predictions or decisions based on input data.

AI-powered Analytics: The integration of AI techniques into data analytics processes to uncover insights, patterns, and trends in large datasets.

Autonomous Agent: An AI system or robot that can perform tasks and make decisions independently without human intervention, often used in robotics and self-driving cars.

Artificial Neural Network (ANN): A computational model inspired by the human brain's neural structure, used for tasks such as pattern recognition and deep learning.

AI Ethics: The study and application of ethical principles in the development and use of artificial intelligence, including considerations of fairness, transparency, and accountability.

AI Governance: The establishment of policies, regulations, and guidelines for the ethical and responsible use of artificial intelligence.

AI Regulation: Government or industry standards and laws governing the development and deployment of AI systems.

AI in Healthcare: The application of AI technologies, such as medical image analysis and predictive analytics, to improve healthcare diagnosis, treatment, and patient care.

AI in Customer Service: The application of AI-powered chatbots and virtual assistants for improving customer support and engagement.

AI in Cybersecurity: The use of AI for threat detection, anomaly detection, and security monitoring in cybersecurity.

AI in Education: The use of AI for personalized learning, intelligent tutoring systems, and automated grading in the education sector.

AI in Energy: The application of AI for energy optimization, grid management, and renewable energy forecasting in the energy industry.

AI in Entertainment: The use of AI for content recommendation, video game design, virtual reality experiences, and personalized entertainment.

AI in Finance: The use of AI for financial tasks like algorithmic trading, risk assessment, fraud detection, and customer service in the finance industry.

AI in Human Resources: The application of AI for tasks like resume screening, candidate matching, and employee engagement analysis in HR processes.

AI in Image Recognition: The use of AI for identifying objects, patterns, and features in images and videos, often used in medical imaging and autonomous vehicles.

AI in Legal Services: The use of AI for tasks like legal document analysis, contract review, and legal research in the legal sector.

AI in Marketing: The application of AI for customer segmentation, targeted advertising, and marketing campaign optimization.

AI in Natural Language Generation (NLG): The use of AI to automatically generate human-like text, often used in content generation and report writing.

AI in Recommender Systems: The use of AI algorithms to provide personalized recommendations for products, content, and services.

AI in Retail: The use of AI for inventory management, demand forecasting, personalized shopping recommendations, and cashierless stores in the retail sector.

AI in Speech Recognition: The application of AI for converting spoken language into text, used in voice assistants and transcription services.

AI in Social Media: The application of AI for content moderation, sentiment analysis, and personalized content recommendations in social media platforms.

AI in Supply Chain Management: The use of AI for optimizing supply chain operations, demand forecasting, and inventory management.

AI in Transportation: The application of AI for tasks like autonomous driving, traffic management, and predictive maintenance in the transportation sector.

AI in Video Analytics: The application of AI for analyzing video content, including object tracking, facial recognition, and event detection.

AI Regulation: Government or industry standards and laws governing the development and deployment of AI systems.

AI Robustness: The ability of AI systems to perform reliably in diverse and challenging environments, including scenarios not seen during training.

AI Transparency: The openness and clarity in the design, development, and operation of AI systems, allowing for external scrutiny and accountability.

Algorithm: A step-by-step procedure or set of rules for solving a particular problem or accomplishing a specific task.

AI in Language Translation: The use of AI for automatic language translation, improving the accuracy and efficiency of translation services.

Anomaly Detection: A machine learning task that identifies unusual or abnormal patterns in data, often used for fraud detection and cybersecurity.

Artificial General Intelligence (AGI): AI systems that possess the ability to understand, learn, and apply knowledge across a wide range of tasks and domains, similar to human intelligence.

Artificial Intelligence (AI): The simulation of human intelligence processes by machines, including learning, reasoning, problem-solving, perception, and language understanding.

BERT (Bidirectional Encoder Representations from Transformers): A pre-trained natural language processing model that has significantly improved performance in various NLP tasks.

Bias in AI: Systematic and unfair discrimination or prejudice in AI algorithms, often related to the quality or representativeness of training data.

Bias Mitigation: The process of reducing or eliminating bias in AI algorithms, often achieved through data preprocessing techniques and algorithmic fairness measures.

Bias-Variance Tradeoff: A fundamental concept in machine learning that refers to the balance between a model's ability to fit the training data (low bias) and generalize to new data (low variance).

Big Data: A term used to describe extremely large and complex datasets that traditional data processing methods are inadequate to handle.

Chatbot: A computer program or AI system designed to engage in text or voice-based conversations with humans.

Chatbot Framework: A set of tools, libraries, and components that simplifies the development of chatbot applications, including natural language understanding and conversation management.

Clustering: An unsupervised learning technique that groups similar data points together based on their inherent characteristics, often used for data exploration.

Computer Vision: The area of AI that aims to teach computers to interpret and understand visual information from the world, including images and videos.

Computer Speech Recognition: The technology that enables computers to convert spoken language into text, often used in voice assistants and transcription services.

Convolutional Neural Network (CNN): A type of neural network commonly used in computer vision tasks, designed to automatically and adaptively learn patterns from data.

Data: Factual information. In the context of AI, it describes extremely large and complex datasets that traditional data processing methods are inadequate to handle.

Data Mining: The process of discovering patterns, trends, and information from large datasets using techniques from machine learning, statistics, and database systems.

Deep Learning: A subfield of machine learning that utilizes artificial neural networks with multiple layers (deep neural networks) to model and solve complex tasks.

Deep Reinforcement Learning: A combination of deep learning and reinforcement learning, used to train AI agents to perform complex tasks.

Dimensionality Reduction: The process of reducing the number of input features in a dataset while retaining important information, commonly used in data preprocessing.

Edge Computing: The practice of processing data locally on edge devices (e.g., IoT devices) rather than sending it to a centralized cloud server, often used for real-time AI applications.

Ensemble Learning: A machine learning technique that combines the predictions of multiple models (e.g., random forests, boosting) to improve overall performance and reduce overfitting.

Ethical AI: The practice of developing AI systems and algorithms that consider ethical and moral implications, avoiding bias, discrimination, and harm to individuals or society.

Ethical AI Audit: An examination and assessment of an AI system's design, development, and deployment to identify potential ethical issues and ensure compliance with ethical standards.

Explainability: The ability to understand and interpret the decisions and predictions made by AI models, especially in complex deep learning models.

Feature Engineering: The process of selecting, creating, or transforming features (input variables) in a dataset to improve the performance of machine learning models.

Federated Learning: A privacy-preserving machine learning approach where model training occurs locally on individual devices or servers, and only model updates are shared centrally.

Generative Adversarial Network (GAN): A type of neural network architecture consisting of two networks, a generator and a discriminator, used for tasks like image generation and style transfer.

Gradient Descent: An optimization algorithm used in machine learning to adjust model parameters iteratively, minimizing the loss function and improving model accuracy.

Hyperparameter: A configuration setting for machine learning algorithms that is set before training and influences the learning process, such as learning rate or the number of hidden layers in a neural network.

Loss Function: A mathematical function that measures the difference between predicted values and actual values, used to train machine learning models.

Machine Learning (ML): A subset of AI that focuses on the development of algorithms and statistical models that enable computer systems to improve their performance on a specific task through learning from data.

Named Entity Recognition (NER): An NLP task that identifies and classifies entities such as names of people, places, organizations, and dates in text data.

Natural Language Processing (NLP): The field of AI that focuses on enabling machines to understand, interpret, and generate human language.

Natural Language Understanding (NLU): A subset of NLP that focuses on the machine's ability to comprehend and extract meaning from human language, often used in chatbots and virtual assistants.

Neural Network: A computational model inspired by the human brain, consisting of interconnected nodes (neurons) organized into layers, used for tasks like pattern recognition and classification.

Overfitting: A common issue in machine learning where a model becomes too specialized in training data and fails to generalize to new, unseen data.

Part-of-Speech Tagging (POS): An NLP task that assigns grammatical tags (e.g., noun, verb, adjective) to words in a sentence.

Preprocessing: The data preparation steps in machine learning, which may include cleaning,

Process Automation (RPA): The use of software robots or "bots" to automate repetitive and rule-based tasks, often used in business processes.

AI-powered Analytics: The integration of AI techniques into data analytics processes to uncover insights, patterns, and trends in large datasets.

Recurrent Neural Network (RNN): A type of neural network suitable for sequential data, where connections between nodes can create loops, allowing for memory of previous inputs.

Quantum Machine Learning: An emerging field that explores the use of quantum computing to enhance machine learning algorithms and solve complex computational problems, transformation, and feature engineering to improve data quality.

Recommender System: An AI system that provides personalized recommendations to users, commonly used in e-commerce, content streaming, and social media platforms.

Recurrent Neural Network (RNN): A type of neural network suitable for sequential data, where connections between nodes can create loops, allowing for memory of previous inputs.

Reinforcement Learning: A machine learning paradigm where agents learn to make decisions through interaction with an environment, maximizing a cumulative reward signal.

Robotic Process Automation (RPA): The use of software robots or "bots" to automate repetitive and rule-based tasks, often used in business processes.

Sentiment Analysis: An NLP task that determines the sentiment or emotional tone expressed in text data, such as positive, negative, or neutral.

Supervised Learning: A machine learning technique where the model is trained on labeled data, and it learns to make predictions based on input features.

Topic Modeling: An NLP technique that identifies and extracts topics or themes from a collection of documents, often used for document clustering and content recommendation.

Transfer Learning: A machine learning technique where a pre-trained model on one task is adapted or fine-tuned for a different but related task, reducing the need for extensive training data.

Unsupervised Learning: A machine learning technique where the model learns patterns and structures from unlabeled data, often used in clustering and dimensionality reduction.

References

AIToolsExplorer. (n.d.) *The history of natural language processing: From ELIZA to GPT*. https://aitoolsexplorer.com/ai-history/the-history-of-natural-language-processing-from-eliza-to-gpt/

Allen, K. (2022, August 25). *How NLP can enhance the metaverse experience*. Acceleration Economy. https://accelerationeconomy.com/metaverse/how-nlp-can-enhance-the-metaverse-experience/

Anastasiadis, S. (2019, April 8). *How is natural language search changing the face of legal research?* Ross. https://blog.rossintelligence.com/post/how-natural-language-search-changing-face-of-legal-research

Anyoha, R. (2017, August 28) *The history of artificial intelligence*. SITN. https://sitn.hms.harvard.edu/flash/2017/history-artificial-intelligence/

Bag, S. (2024, February 20). *Master natural language processing in 2022 with best resources*. Analytics Vidhya. https://www.analyticsvidhya.com/blog/2022/01/master-natural-language-processing-in-2022-with-best-resources/

Benotti, L., & Blackburn, P. (2022). *Ethics consideration sections in natural language processing papers*. ACL Anthology. https://aclanthology.org/2022.emnlp-main.299.pdf

Bloomberg Professional Services. (2023, March 30). *Introducing BloombergGPT, Bloomberg's 50-billion parameter large language model, purpose-built from scratch for finance*. Bloomberg. https://www.bloomberg.com/company/press/bloomb erggpt-50-billion-parameter-llm-tuned-finance/

Brownlee, J. (2019, August 7). *A gentle introduction to neural machine translation*. Machine Learning Mastery. https://machinelearningmastery.com/introduction-neural-machine-translation/

Caliskan, A. (2021, May 10). *Detecting and mitigating bias in natural language processing*. Brookings. https://www.brookings.edu/articles/detecting-and-mitigating-bias-in-natural-language-processing/

Codecademy Team. (n.d.). *Ethics of chatbots*. Codecademy. https://www.codecademy.com/article/ethics-of-chatbots

Dawson, B. (2023, May 25). *Unintended consequences and data privacy concerns in the age of AI*. McDonald Hopkins. https://www.mcdonaldhopkins.com/insights/news/unintended-consequences-and-data-privacy-concerns-in-the-age-of-ai

Foote, K. (2023, July 6). *A brief history of natural language processing*. Dataversity. https://www.dataversity.net/a-brief-history-of-natural-language-processing-nlp/

Gruetzemacher, R. (2022, April 19). *The power of natural language processing*. Harvard Business Review. https://hbr.org/2022/04/the-power-of-natural-language-processing

Hao, K. (2024, March 1). *AI is taking water from the desert*. Atlantic Monthly. https://www.theatlantic.com/technology/archive/2024/03/ai-water-climate-microsoft/677602/

Hingrajia, M. (2023, September 27). *Step-by-step guide on building a chatbot using DialogFlow.* Maruti Techlabs. https://marutitech.com/build-a-chatbot-using-dialogflow/

IBM. (n.d.). *What is natural language processing (NLP)?* IBM. https://www.ibm.com/topics/natural-language-processing

Ivey, A. (2023, April 25). *5 real-world applications of natural language processing.* CoinTelegraph. https://cointelegraph.com/news/5-real-world-applications-of-natural-language-processing-nlp

Larkin, Z. (2022, November 16). *General AI vs narrow AI.* Levity. https://levity.ai/blog/general-ai-vs-narrow-ai

Leigh, A. (n.d.). *6 uses for natural language processing in healthcare.* Hitachi Solutions. https://global.hitachi-solutions.com/blog/nlp-in-healthcare/

Kadlaskar, A. (2024, February 26). *Natural language processing step by step.* Analytics Vidhya. https://www.analyticsvidhya.com/blog/2021/05/natural-language-processing-step-by-step-guide/

Kotek, H., Dockum, R., & Sun, D. (2023). *Gender bias and stereotypes in Large Language Models.* MIT Libraries. https://dspace.mit.edu/handle/1721.1/153131

Kublik, S., & Saboo, S. (2022, May). *A beginner's guide to GPT-3.* Datacamp. https://www.datacamp.com/blog/a-beginners-guide-to-gpt-3

Kumar, M. (n.d.). *Limitations & challenges of using GPT 3: An overview.* CronJ. https://www.cronj.com/blog/limitations-challenges-of-using-gpt-3-an-overview/

Maderis, G. (2024, January 25). *Top 22 benefits of chatbots for businesses and customers.* Zendesk. https://www.zendesk.com/blog/5-benefits-using-ai-bots-customer-service/

Mishra, S. (2021, December 21). *5 applications of NLP in education.* AnalyticSteps. https://www.analyticssteps.com/blogs/applications-nlp-education

MonkeyLearn. (n.d.). *Natural language processing (NLP): 7 key techniques.* https://monkeylearn.com/blog/natural-language-processing-techniques/

MonkeyLearn. (n.d.). *Learn how to do sentiment analysis with deep learning.* https://monkeylearn.com/blog/sentiment-analysis-deep-learning/

MonkeyLearn. (n.d.). *Major challenges of natural language processing.* https://monkeylearn.com/blog/natural-language-processing-challenges/

Orza, P. (2022, November 16). 11 real-life examples of NLP in action. Levity. https://levity.ai/blog/11-nlp-real-life-examples

Pearl, M. (2023, June 1). *This children's hospital is integrating AI with healthcare.* Mashable. https://mashable.com/article/ai-healthcare-integration

Raj, N. (2023, November 6). *Sentiment analysis in natural language processing.* Analytics Vidhya. https://www.analyticsvidhya.com/blog/2021/06/nlp-sentiment-analysis/

Rashid, T. (2016). *Make Your Own Neural Network.* CreateSpace.

Scuotto, I. (2022, February 22). *Natural language processing chatbot: NLP in a nutshell.* Landbot. https://landbot.io/blog/natural-language-processing-chatbot

Sharma, S. (2023, June 12). *Top 10 applications of sentiment analysis in business.* Analytics Vidhya. https://www.analyticsvidhya.com/blog/2023/01/top-10-applications-of-sentiment-analysis-in-business/

Sharwood, S. (2023, September 21). *Authors Guild sues OpenAI for using Game of Thrones and other novels to train ChatGPT.* The Register. https://www.theregister.com/2023/09/21/authors_guild_openai_lawsuit/

Shrivastava, V. (2024, February 22). *Innovation unleashed: The hottest NLP technologies of 2022.* Analytics Vidhya. https://www.analyticsvidhya.com/blog/2022/12/innovation-unleashed-the-hottest-nlp-technologies-of-2022/

Stoyanov, V., & Ayan, N. (2018, January 25). *Under the hood: Multilingual embeddings.* Meta. https://ai.meta.com/blog/under-the-hood-multilingual-embeddings/

Tatwadarshi, P. (2024, January 24). *Role of machine learning in natural language processing.* Analytics Vidhya. https://www.analyticsvidhya.com/blog/2021/04/role-of-machine-learning-in-natural-language-processing/

TDS. (2017, June 7). *Five practical use cases of customer sentiment analysis.* Medium. https://towardsdatascience.com/five-practical-use-cases-of-customer-sentiment-analysis-for-nps-a3167ac2caaa

Thorn, J. (2021, July 19). *The challenges, recent advances, and future of deep learning.* Medium.

https://medium.com/geekculture/the-challenges-recent-advances-and-future-of-deep-learning-d714304656b

Valera, N. (2023, April 24). *The challenges and opportunities of neural machine translation*. Talkao. https://talkao.com/blog/the-challenges-and-opportunities-of-neural-machine-translation/

Vaswani, A., Shazeer, N., Parmar, N., Uszkoreit, J., Jones, L., Gomez, A., Kaiser, L., & Polosukhin, I. (2017, June 12). Attention is all you need. *arXiv*. https://doi.org/10.48550/arXiv.1706.03762

Wang, Z. (2023, April 13). *How and why transformer models transformed NLP*. Deepgram. https://deepgram.com/learn/capturing-attention-decoding-the-success-of-transformer-models-in-natural-language-processing

Wankhade, M., Rao, A., & Kulkarni, C. (2022, February 7). A survey on sentiment analysis methods, applications, and challenges. *Artificial Intelligence Review, 55*, 5731–5780. https://doi.org/10.1007/s10462-022-10144-1

Welocalize. (2022, March 10). *The role of NLP in global communications*. https://www.welocalize.com/nlp-in-global-communications/

Worswick, S. (n.d.). *Designing an ethical chatbot*. InfoQ. https://www.infoq.com/presentations/designing-chatbot-ethics/

www.ingramcontent.com/pod-product-compliance
Lightning Source LLC
LaVergne TN
LVHW012022060526
838201LV00061B/4411